Power Marketing

Taking your Business to the Next Level

By Gráinne Farrell

Copyright © Gráinne Farrell 2021

Contents

Introduction

"The sales are just not coming in."

"Our revenues are too low."

"We are barely tapping into the potential out there."

"Why are people not buying our product?"

"We have an excellent service, but people are just not interested."

"We have a much better product than our competitors, yet they have a much larger market share."

"Why do they keep winning the tenders when we could do a much better job?"

Do any of these statements sound familiar to you? Do you hear and say them weekly, if not daily? Let us flip each scenario.

"The sales are through the roof."

"Our revenues are beginning to grow."

"We have really captured the market."

"It is great that so many people are buying our products."

"We are seeing high levels of our audience engaging in what we do."

"We are way ahead of our competitors when it comes to market share." "Our success rate at winning tenders just keeps growing."

"We are so glad that our target audience understands the value of our products."

How would you feel if you could say these statements truthfully every day? Would it make a big difference to your current situation?

Would it be a game-changer for your business? If the answer is yes, then you have come to the right place. This book will help those businesses who either do not have a marketing person in-house or a company that employs a marketing person or marketing team but feel that the business is not making progress. Adapting the strategies in this book will help raise your brand awareness, increase your online engagement, increase your market share, and generate larger revenues.

There seems to be a huge gap in how marketing is perceived and how it should be. I am here to bridge that gap. Some businesses view marketing as an expensive cost without understanding the potential financial return when applied effectively.

Some readers may have some marketing experience but want to strengthen their knowledge.

Experienced marketeers will be familiar with a lot of the content in this book, but they will benefit from the examples and guidance I offer. It will help them view situations and approaches differently.

This book is very much based on practical advice from my near twenty years in the Marketing industry, working with small to medium enterprises and large companies nationally and internationally. If your product is not selling and you do not know why I will help you change that. If you feel you have a great service but cannot understand why you are not generating more interest, I will help you generate the interest. If your business is in trouble and you are considering ceasing to trade, this book could help you do a complete turnaround and become a market leader.

If you are spending a large portion of your budget on marketing with limited results, I can help you invest your budget to get the return you require.

This book will help you generate the revenues you know you can deliver. Small to Medium companies and Start-ups are the ones that usually benefit from my help the most. This book will resonate more with people from those backgrounds. Larger companies tend to have sufficient marketing teams capable of driving the company where it needs to go.

That is not to say this book cannot help the larger corporations. It certainly can, especially with market segmentation and target marketing.

I have a quite diverse background globally and nationally, including gaming, software, energy, insurance, and recycling. I have a first-class degree in Business, I am a certified Digital Marketing Professional and have been involved in some substantial partnerships, including working with Manchester United Football Club, Ladbrokes, and World Series of Poker.

I decided to write this book to help those who really want to drive their business forward but are not making progress or getting their desired results. It is for those out there who know they have an excellent product or service but find things are just not happening for them, or they feel revenues should be much higher. It could be that they should have a much larger market share but are barely chipping into that potential. Maybe a business or company feels stuck and cannot see a way forward. Maybe you want to improve your image in the hope that, in time, you will be bought out by a larger company for a lucrative price, but currently the interest is not forthcoming.

Every Marketeer has their own approach to what they do. And that is to be respected. My approach is very straight forward, to the point and with none of the fluffy stuff. I tell it how it is. And everything I share is based on my own experiences.

So, if you are on board, we will kick off and begin the process of propelling your business forward and taking it to the next level.

Knowing how to speak to your target market is of the utmost importance. Unfortunately, this is where a lot of companies fall at the first hurdle. Target marketing will be a prominent part of this book.

If I went to a car dealer and asked the salesperson about the latest Ford SUV, I would expect them to tell me about the features, the size, petrol or diesel, automatic, electric windows, sunroof, and all the items I would understand.

However, if they started to talk about the different parts of the engine—the catalytic converter, the new head gasket, the heat pumps—I would be looking at them questioningly. Sometimes when companies advertise their products, they have become so familiar with them that their advert campaigns can be the equivalent of a car advert highlighting a head gasket, a heat pump, and a catalytic converter. My point being, you need to think of your customer, the people who you are trying to attract. Looking at your own adverts. Would a person who knows nothing of you or your company immediately recognize what you are selling? And would the benefits you outline in the advert resonate with them?

It is vital to remember that while you may understand your product inside out, the potential customer may not.

And chances are, they do not want to. They are just interested in what it can do to benefit them and know that they will be happy with that purchase. Understanding *why* your customers buy your product, and not why you *think* they buy your product, is key. Once you have that information, it makes marketing campaigns much more targeted, successful, and most importantly, cost-effective.

Chapter One – Vision/Company Objectives

Before we move on, please think about your company or the business you are in, or the company you work for, whatever the situation may be, or whatever the reason you are reading this.

Create a personal or company vision – what is a company vision though? It is a vision that gives a vivid mental image of where you want your business (or you) to be at some point in the future, based on your goals and aspirations.

Companies that succeed stay true to their values over the years and create a business that employees and customers are proud to associate with. So be sure to create a vision if you have not yet done so. But do not make it an easy goal. Do not limit yourself.

You should NOT do the following:

Say to yourself, "I would like to have a national car dealership with a new glass-front garage and have the franchise for the Ford model," and then stop for a moment, and say, "No, actually, I'll never be able to win a franchise, nor get that type of garage. Ah, sure, once I am selling cars and making money I'll be happy!" This is a big no. Do not underestimate yourself and your business. The first half of this statement was an excellent vision; don't ruin it by doubting yourself.

You should be confident in your role or in what you have created. Once you have carved out your vision for yourself or your company, then you need to work out your objectives. What do I need to achieve for my vision to be realized?

Are there certain areas you want to develop? Do you want to increase your product offerings? Do you want to keep doing what you are doing but increase market share?

Have a good think about this. You will likely have plans tucked away at the back of your mind. Now is the time to take them out, study them, and decide what you want for your business long term.

If you are just managing your company day to day and not really worrying about the future, it is challenging to groom your business to become a market leader.

Before I move on, if parts of this book do not apply to your business, just read them and move on. Do not overthink anything. I am offering guidance to help all companies. Business to Business, Business to Consumer, Online, and Traditional. Once you get the marketing framework correct, it can then be applied to any business in any industry sector. Towards the end of the book, I will include chapters specifically on the next steps you should take, broken down into Sole Trader and SMEs, with some information about Larger Corporations.

We will cover everything before we get to those chapters so that you will have a much better understanding of marketing when we do get to the next steps.

You may have a marketing person or a marketing team already in situ. This will give you a great advantage in terms of being able work with them to follow the advice in this book. Even if you are someone who will not be doing any of the initiatives yourself, this book will give you greater insight into what your marketing team could be doing differently, and it will help you liaise with and guide them if necessary.

I have been very budget conscious while writing this book. The information I am giving you are the basics you should be doing. We will pick the minimum steps you need to take to get started. These will be outlined in the chapters towards the end. If you stick to the plan, your business has the potential to be a Market Leader in no time!

Please note when reading this book, the information I provide is solely based on my own experience. My guidance and advice will get you to where you want to be. If there are other marketing initiatives that you would like to try that I may not have covered, please do so. Just make sure that whatever you are doing is in line with your newly created marketing strategy. Make sure it fits in nicely and complements what you are already actioning. If someone is doing it for you, make sure they are also aware of your marketing strategy to align it to initiatives you have already planned. I do not specialize in one specific area; I advise on the whole marketing spectrum. This is how you will benefit the most.

If you want to learn more about a specific area within my book, there is lots of great information available in journals, online, or books that go into more detail. You will be better positioned after reading this to judge if you are happy enough to get started or whether you want to find out more about specific topics—whatever feels right for you.

The main thing you will take away from this book is that you will have a much better understanding of marketing. You will understand which marketing initiative to use to achieve your different goals, you will understand the importance of speaking directly to your target audience and why market segmentation is so important on your journey to becoming a Market Leader!

Chapter Two – Market Segmentation & Target Marketing

From experience, I have often heard statements like: "Oh, the website is not important" or "It's only a sign for the local football pitch" or "Ah, it's just an advert for the local paper". Everything matters when your potential audience can see it. You never know who might be watching or what opportunities might lie in wait. To put your best foot forward, everything should be kept aligned and consistent. They are all linked together and they all complement each other. Aligning your business will portray a professional image at every angle. It also puts you in the right frame of mind for moving forward. The more professional you come across the more opportunities will come your way.

[1]*Strategybeam, a leading marketing consulting firm, states that "defining the target market for your business is the most important piece of digital marketing. By understanding your target market, you can set your marketing efforts and direct your business operations toward success."*

Let us start with this. Ask yourself the questions outlined below. Be clear in your mind what the answers should be. It will make the rest of the book much more beneficial if you can apply your current situation to the rest of the book's information and guidance. You can write it down if it's easier or keep the answers in your head to apply them to the different scenarios when they arise.

    (a) What? —What is your product or service? If you have many, start with the main one or pick the most profitable. For marketing to be most effective, each individual product or service needs a different strategy. So just start with one.

---

[1]

(b) Who? —Who buys this product? Think of their age, gender, occupation, interests, disposable income, etc. You most likely have two to three different types, which can be put into groups.

(c) Why? —Why do they buy your product? What value does it offer them? What are the benefits for them in buying your product?

(d) Where? —Where are your customers from? Are they local, national or global?

Now, these groups you have identified are known as segments. When I refer to segments, remember it is a specific type of customer who buys your products.

Here is an example. If your company provided electronic items and wanted to advertise a new slick pair of headphones, you could potentially have many groups if you were to start segmenting your whole audience. But to make it simple, we will demonstrate just three. Let's say from the research we know that: -

> Group/Segment 1 – Teenagers/young adults would use these headphones to listen to music/play games/group chats.

> Group/Segment 2 – Middle-aged men and women who listen to music when working out would use these headphones.

> Group/Segment 3 – Older generation who listen to audiobooks would use these headphones.

Each segment has a different reason why they might purchase the headphones. We need to use this information. Rather than creating one advert to target all these groups together, create three separate adverts.

Advert Possibilities

Segment 1 – Teenagers – Advert 1 shows teenagers having a good time with headphones on, enjoying music, dancing, laughing, etc. This image would appeal to that segment and when they see the advert; they would likely engage with it.

Segment 2 – Middle-aged men and women – Advert 2 shows a man or a woman running on a treadmill or out for a jog while listening to headphones. This would appeal to this segment.

Segment 3 – The older generation – Advert 3 shows an older person sitting back relaxing in a chair, listening to an audiobook. With a clear heading, "Listen to your audiobook in comfort."

Three separate adverts for the same product targeted directly at each segment. Consider this: an old age pensioner who loves to read but her eyesight is not great or reading gives her a headache. This person receives a leaflet or sees an advert for headphones with young people listening to music or adults with headphones on while working out. Do you think the headphones would interest the older woman? Most likely not.
Unless she was a super ninja granny who worked out every day. However, if she saw the advert showing someone her own age using the headphones to listen to audiobooks, do you think she might be

interested? She most likely would. She would be delighted. She has found a solution to her problem!

And that is the key to marketing. Find out how you can help your target audience and dress the solution up in an advert specifically targeted at them. So not only do they want to buy your product, but they are also happy to do so.

You can see how much more likely each target audience would be to click the advert relevant to them, rather than to have one that covers all. There will be a much higher engagement rate when there is an advert for each group. This does not just apply to online adverts. It can cover TV and radio too— the advert's content should depend on who the audience for each station are. The same goes for magazines or newspapers. Who is reading them? Find out the demographics of the people exposed to your adverts and create content that will interest them. This is how to get the most out of your marketing budget. You are investing in campaigns that are directly targeted to your audiences.

And, therefore, you are not wasting your budget by showing adverts to people who will have no interest in them, no matter how good they look or sound.

As an example, I previously ran a campaign for a make-up school which had a new course they wanted to advertise. Their audience ranged from school leavers up to women in their sixties. We broke the campaign down into three segments. One was targeted at young schoolgirls. We created exciting looking adverts highlighting how they could have a career in the fashion industry or the movie industry as a make-up artist. Then we targeted people in their twenties or thirties who always wanted to be make-up artists but had never taken the leap. We focused on adverts such as: "Unleash your potential—do it today". The third group focused on people who had full-time jobs but might want to do make-up artistry on the side as a second income. By creating these three separate advert campaigns, we were inundated with messages from people wanting more information.

We had a very successful response rate and secured many bookings. Those who did not book the course initially, asked to be kept updated on any future courses when they arose. Compared with previous campaigns that used a one advert fits all approach, this one gained a vastly higher engagement rate.

Target Marketing

We need to get the images right for our adverts— and the messaging. Imagine yourself in the mind of the person you are trying to sell to in each group. Who are they? Why are they buying your product?

If you were that person, what would you want to hear before you bought the item? Or better still, what would convince you to buy the product straight away? Never make assumptions based on what you think. Always put yourself in their shoes, or if you are not good at visualization, use a focus group. Or phone some friends or family who would fall into the segment you are targeting and ask for their opinions.

You are attracting each segment by using messages that they want to hear—that is key. If you market the product in the right way that speaks to each audience directly, you can greatly increase your customer base. You must create a different marketing strategy for each audience. Do not let that scare you or think that there is too much work involved. It is straightforward to do once you get the hang of it. For example, I am in the catering business and I want to promote my services to sports teams for after-match functions.

Let us say I create a leaflet that shows beautifully arranged sandwiches on plates, bowls of cocktails sausages and chicken wings, trays of wraps and salads.

Now if we were to take Gaelic football and tennis in this case. Two very different audiences. The chances are, if the football club representative looked at the leaflet, they would think, "That's great. They look nice. Let's order." And that would be it, with little thought being given. Based on my experience, after a football match people are just delighted to have a sandwich with a nice cup of tea and how the sandwiches look or are presented is not important to them as long as they taste good.

Take tennis, however,—a totally different ball game. Excuse the pun! And again, this is based on my experience and no offence intended. I love both sports and both cultures.

But when it comes to the after-match spread at a tennis match, you would be better to envision the Queen coming to afternoon tea. There is nearly more competition for the food spread after the games than there is on the court.

So, back to my leaflet. If a food leaflet such as I described earlier came through the tennis club door, I have no doubt it would be popped straight into the recycling bin without so much as a glance.

Why? Because we are dealing with an audience with different preferences. Does that mean the catering business service will not be successful in the tennis industry? Absolutely not. We just need to speak the audience language. So how do we go about it and reach these people?

We should create visual content and messaging that will attract this market segment. If you research what tennis teams like to offer after games, you will find items such as salmon on brown bread, crackers, cheese, salad sandwiches, home-baked desserts, quiche, salami, grapes, maybe some nuts, and so on. Do you see the difference? Can the caterer supply this? Absolutely. Sending a leaflet to a tennis club with this type of food pictured would have a much greater chance of success than the one we first referred to. It really IS just about tailoring the product or service to the specific audience it is serving. It sounds simple because it is.

[2]*"Our jobs as marketers are to understand how the customer wants to buy and help them to do so."* states Bryan Eisenberg who is a recognized authority and pioneer in online marketing.

This highlights the absolute importance of understanding why a certain customer might buy your product or service. This leads to another example.

I use many examples as it is much easier to explain and get the message across when you can understand how a situation develops. It is easier to process the information and have a reference, "Ah, yes, I need to do x, y, or z here."

There is little effect in creating generic campaigns that give out one message to a whole target audience. That is not to say that your campaign will not be successful. It could be. You could do quite well and, let us say, get a 2% click-through rate. However, if you segment your market and created individual campaigns, you may have an overall click rate of 10%. By keeping it generic, you are losing out on potential sales. A lot of companies do this and are not aware that they are diluting their message.

Think about this: if a casino sends a poker promotion to all its members, how many of those will be interested? A casino has many segments: blackjack, roulette, slots, tournaments, and so on. Targeting all members or potential members with a poker promotion will only attract those who like poker. You might say, "So what? They are still getting the message, right?" Right. However, there are two important points to note here.

2

Number one: the cost. It will be much more costly as you are trying to reach all your audience at one time, and the message will be lost on the majority of those you are trying to target. Therefore, 70% of your investment could likely go down the drain.

Whereas, if you divided the one campaign into two or three segments, all with different messages relating to each target audience's interests, it would be much more cost-effective. 100% of your audience are seeing a message that interests them.

And number two. If I am a slot player and continuously get messages about poker, roulette, and other games, it is likely I will stop taking an interest in your promotions. You are, in effect, going to annoy me in the long run. When you do have a good promotion that I am be interested in, I may not even open the email or the text or whatever it may be. I will have formed an opinion that your messages usually do not relate to my interests—this is where the damage is done. This is how companies invest a lot in marketing but receive little back in return. On the other hand, if you divide the market into segments and target them with relevant content, people are much more likely to open or notice your message as it speaks directly to them. And your investment will be much more rewarding and profitable.

Does that mean I cannot cross-market my other products? No, certainly not. We must create effective strategies to cross market efficiently. We will cover cross marketing later in the book.

When I was working in the UK, many moons ago, we were posting out (posting in the actual post. Yes, as I said, many moons ago) free bets to slot, roulette, and poker players.

They were all segmented based on preferences and we were generating good results. However, after receiving an angry phone call from an irate customer, we realized our mistake.

We were sending out £5 bets to all our customers, relevant to whatever game they preferred. What we did not consider was how valuable the customer was. What do I mean by that? For example, some people might spend £20 or £30 on a visit to a casino whereas others might spend £20,000 to £30,000. Imagine spending thousands in one night then receiving a free £5 bet in the post a couple of days later. It wouldn't really mean much, would it? And this goes for all businesses. Some customers will spend little with you and some a lot.

If you are running a promotion, keep in mind that the offer must be appropriate for those clients or customers who will receive it.

Considering everything discussed so far, look at your past marketing campaigns, current website, social media platforms, adverts you are running, or email campaigns. How do you feel about them now? Are you happy that your marketing material is speaking directly to those it is intended for? You can most likely see a gap in your marketing versus your audience preferences. If you can see it, you can fix it. Remember what needs to be done and please do not worry about how you will go about all this. At the end of this book, I will provide a step-by-step process to creating a successful marketing strategy for your business.

When creating visuals, it is worth the investment to create a Content Bank or a Gallery. This should be made up of different types of adverts in different formats. Depending on the size of your company, you may have an in-house graphic person or even a marketing agency already. If not, hiring a freelance graphic designer and giving them a detailed account of what you need will be worth it. Then, whenever you are starting a campaign, you will already have the visuals on hand. You may simply have to change the wording and messaging either yourself or with the help of the freelance graphic designer. Either way, you should create a visual content bank—crisp, clear images with your company logo and somewhere to add the text. Although there needs to be an array of different images, there should still be some consistency across the board. Keep them similar in style. Always use the same text font and present the contact information in the same format.

[3]*Brian Clark, a successful writer and the founder of the pioneering content marketing website, Copyblogger, says, " On average, 8 out of 10 people will read your headline copy, but only 2 out 10 will read the rest."*

Keep this in mind. Keep it simple. And make sure the headline is effective enough to give the reader the message you intended to give them.

Keep the overall look and feel the same.

Consistency is key. It represents professionalism and gives an organized image. There is nothing worse than seeing adverts made up with wording all over the place with too much information, and logos being used in different colours and formats. They are ugly and give off a disorganized message. Little information is better than too much information. Less is more.

The main goal should be to deliver one specific message that will direct the person to a website or webpage, or shop to find out more. Create a crisp advert with refreshing imagery, and clean, clear wording, with one message.

There must be a CALL to ACTION. A call to action is something that gives someone an instruction. All adverts should always include a clear, easy-to-see CALL TO ACTION. Examples:

DOWNLOAD NOW - CLICK HERE - SIGN UP TODAY - FIND OUT MORE - BUY NOW - WATCH NOW

> "Lose two pounds a week – **Watch How Here**." (link to video). Highlight a Benefit (Recommended by Experts) That should be it with a logo and an image.

3

> "Want a new kitchen? Can't afford one? We can help You" - Use a nice image and logo. Highlight a benefit (Free Consultation). Call to Action "**FIND OUT HOW**" with a link to more information.

> "New to Poker? Not sure how to Play? It's easy with our New Game – **Download Now**!" Keep it simple.

When you are happy with your visual gallery, you should update your company image across all platforms using these new visuals. Use two or three of them on the homepage of your website as the homepage slider banner. Use them on your Facebook profile page and your Twitter, Instagram, LinkedIn, and so on, changing every couple of months.

Keep in mind the audience of each platform. Facebook can be generic enough as it is a tool most people use. But LinkedIn is business-related, so choose a visual image that has a corporate look and message. If you have a fleet of vehicles, look at rebranding your fleet with your new visuals. Yes, it is an investment, but a worthwhile one. It is free advertising and, if done right, is very effective.

If you have current signs or other marketing materials, you should rebrand them to look consistent. This is the foundation of building your brand image. If your logo is on it, rebrand it.

It does not portray well when a company has different adverts or promotional material made of different logos, colouring, and messaging. It does not instill confidence in people and certainly does not display professionalism. Which leads me on to the next topic.

Your Logo and Tagline

Let us start with your logo. Is it clean, crisp, clear? Or is it old fashioned, dull, and maybe a little boring? I am not recommending that you change your logo completely or get a new one but there is no harm in making a few subtle changes for the better. Look at other companies' logos—the leaders. Look at companies in other countries to give you a fresh perspective. Do a little research. If you are on stage accepting an award at a black-tie event and your logo was up in bright lights on a large screen, would you be proud of it? Do you think the audience would be impressed? Think about it. Get your team involved. Get some feedback.

Do not take constructive feedback personally. If suggestions are made to change a logo, advert or tagline, never be offended. It is not personal—it is to help. Accept the help and move on or you will find it difficult to progress to the next level. Look at things from other points of view and make the changes you need with a positive attitude.

Tagline – what is a tagline? It is a motto, so to speak. A **tagline** is a catchy phrase that creates an image of your brand in your customers' minds. Some examples:

- ❖ Greenstar Recycling – setting the standard
- ❖ Tesco – every little helps
- ❖ Toyota – The best built cars in the world
- ❖ McDonald's – i'm lovin' it
- ❖ Nike – JUST DO IT.
- ❖ Maybelline – Maybe she's born with it. Maybe it's Maybelline.

These are all large companies, some global, but that does not mean that your business should not have a tagline. If it does already, great but make sure it is fit for purpose. If you do not have a tagline, get one. I am sure you often sponsor local events or do the odd advert here and there for local sports teams and the like. Maybe it is more than that. Maybe your logo is out there a lot. Taglines, for me, are most important when your logo is appearing on its own. They are not so important when featuring in an advert, as you can usually tell what is being sold or what the company is about.

However, if I see a company logo I haven't seen before featured somewhere, I will have no idea what that company does unless there is a good tagline. The tagline gives you the chance to let people know immediately what you do and provides the chance to instill confidence with your target audience. Large brands get away with having a logo that just enhances their brand. They do not need to tell people what they do, as the world already knows. The likes of "Just do it" "I'm Lovin' It" "Every Little Helps" are worthwhile taglines as people recognize how they relate to that company. Now, if your company name already describes what you do, this type of tagline would also work for you. For example, if you have a car dealership called "Premium Motors", people would know what industry you were in. "Payroll Solutions" would tell people that your business is payroll related. Something generic like "Your trusted partner" would work here. However, if you were a payroll company called "Chapley" and you had "Your trusted partner", people would not know what you were a trusted partner in. However, that is easily fixed. You could have

"Chapley – Your trusted partner in payroll software!" Now people know what you do and you are adding confidence with it!

Have a look at your current tagline and ask yourself if it tells people who do not know you what you do? If it does, great. If not, look at rewording it. Do some research. Again, look up taglines. There are thousands available online that you can browse through. Send some options to your family and friends and get their feedback. Find one you like, tailor it to your business and once you have done this, get your graphic designer to remodel your logo to include this new tagline! And boom—it's done. It all adds up. Everything complements each other. When everything is done consistently, and in alignment, that is when you will begin to see the rewards. [4]*An article on forbes.com states, "A good tagline helps set you apart from other companies that provide similar products."*

Content

So let's you have all visuals consistent, displaying the messaging you want and you have your different market segments identified for each product. You have started running custom campaigns that speak directly to each target segment. This should make an immense difference in your marketing campaigns, and you should start to see positive results. To stand out and gain more market share, and to be viewed as a market leader, you must demonstrate leadership.

You must show you are knowledgeable in the market. To do that, you must put out information relevant to your industry in the form of articles, press releases, videos, whitepapers, presentations, and so much more. Not sure you can do that? Yes, you can.

And this will be the easiest part. From my experience, companies usually know their industry inside out. They know everything, including how products have developed, new technologies in the industries, what competitors are up to, technical product knowledge, and so on. I would likely say most of you reading this are the same. Whether you are in the car sales business, insurance, beauty, software, furniture, architecture, whatever it may be, I'm sure you

---

4

know your business inside out. Right? Then why not get it out there. You would be surprised at the number of people interested in what you have to say.

You must remember, YOU know your industry inside out but those you are selling to do not.

It is like marketing for me. I am confident there is not much I do not know about the subject but when I meet with clients, I realise there is so much they do not know. Things that appear so obvious to me make no sense to my clients, and it is the same with your business. You may know how to draw architectural plans, what details are needed, what technology to use, and what to do and what not to do. But If you were to ask me, I would not have a clue.

Which is why I would use the service of an architect.

My point here is, use language and examples that someone like me, who knows nothing about your business, would understand. Just as I am doing with here with marketing for you.

I have no doubt you could all write a book on your business, such is your level of knowledge of it. So, use this knowledge.

[5]*Jay Bear, one of the world's most inspirational marketing and customer experience keynote speakers, says, "Grow Your Business by Helping, Not Selling."*

Offer good content that solves a problem or answers a question that a potential customer may have. Share information that will help. Do not treat this as a sales pitch. It is not. As you continue to release information about your industry and give people tips, you will build your credibility and be recognized as an industry leader. You will begin to get calls to do talks at events and asked for interviews in magazines. This process takes time and patience but it works and it will get you to where you want to go. Put the effort in, and you will be rewarded.

5

Examples

A car dealership

Offer tips on what to look for when buying a brand-new car or buying a used car. Offer tips on how long to keep a car for or the most effective way to remove stains from the seats. Showcase new cars that have just arrived on your forecourt, capturing the interior and exterior on video, not as a sales pitch—just as information. Create a video of someone offering these tips, write a blog piece, write it as a news story, and so on. Use three to four different formats and release one a week on each platform.

Software

If you have a type of software, come up with tips to help people who could potentially use your software. For example, suppose you have payroll software. Offer five tips on organizing employees and pay-slips. Or five tips on how to effectively manage holidays and time off.

Architects

If you have an architectural firm, offer five tips on what people stumble upon the most when creating plans for houses or buildings. Offer tips on the best area to put your utility room or the best area to have your staff canteen.

Builders

If you are a builder, give other builders tips about how to do things more effectively. If there are difficult areas that all builders are aware of and dislike doing, give tips on the best way to approach the jobs everyone hates.

<u>Beauty</u>

Create videos of make-up applications, focusing on different facial parts. One video could be about lipstick and lip liner, another could be about the eyes and using eyeshadows and eyeliner effectively. Demo someone getting their nails done and offer tips on some exciting designs.

The easiest way to establish what tips people might be interested in is to ask yourself, "What are the most common questions prospective customers ask me?" Then, if you provide this information before it's asked, you are effectively removing a barrier to sale for them. From a business-to-business perspective, think to yourself, "What are the most important things a business looks for from us when we are negotiating?" And from this, create a video, article, or whitepaper on those areas. It means that when these materials are read, your potential customers already know what you can offer without having to ask you, which raises your credibility and puts you in with a great chance of being a serious contender on the tender list.

By releasing all this content over time, your target market is much more aware of your brand and now think of you as a leader in your field. When they need the type of service you provide, you should make it to the top of the tender list or be chosen by a household every time as it is your company that they associate the product with. When your company decides to run promotions, they will be much more effective, given all the content you have been sharing before the campaigns.

People will be more confident about your product and your company and feel you know what you are talking about. You are a safe purchase.

[6]"*Content marketing is more than a buzzword. It is the hottest trend in marketing because it is the biggest gap between what buyers want and brands produce.*" *Michael Brenner.* Michael Brenner is a globally recognized keynote speaker on leadership, culture, and marketing.

Perception is key

The thing that stands out most for me in my nearly twenty years of marketing experience is the importance of PERCEPTION. How the market sees a company, how they are perceived, can make or break a business. Let us explore this theory —let's take two hair salons.

Hair salon one has a great team of hairdressers: they all get on brilliantly, there is a lovely atmosphere in the place, and customers keep going back because they feel so well looked after. They are busy every day, and the business is making a decent profit.

Hair salon two have only one or two bookings a day. The team there are not happy. There is a frosty atmosphere in the place and customers cannot warm to the staff or the salon. The business is not generating a profit and is very near to closing its doors.

Hair salon one is so busy they don't have time to post on social media. They have a Facebook page but hardly ever share anything. They also have a website, but it was launched years ago and is never updated. They figure, why should we bother? They are in a good place with plenty of business coming in.

Hair salon two regularly post on Facebook, Instagram, and their YouTube channel. There is not a day that goes by that there are no

---

6

pictures or videos of cool hair, new styles or staff having fun. They have a modern website suitable for mobiles and have a section with videos and articles for people to access tips for the beauty industry.

The Perception

I am from a film production company, or a large department store, or a leading wedding event management company. I am on the lookout for a really sharp, modern salon that is up to date with hair, make-up and nails, and everything else that goes with it. E.g. tanning, waxing, you get the picture. I have started following different salons on social media to get a feel for them and see how they are received in the market. I check out the websites and have a look at their content. Do you see where I am going with this? Straight away, salon two gives off the best perception by far, not just outdoing hair salon one but outdoing all the rest. They are by far the most proactive on social media; the content they post is exciting and really resonates with their target audience.

They receive loads of comments and shares on their pictures and videos and just seem to be that step ahead of the rest.

The Opportunity

I am going to contact salon two and see if they would be interested in working with us.

We would be offering them an extremely lucrative contract, which could change everything for that salon owner in seconds and somersault their business forward, achieving profits they had only dreamed of.

Now, if I were to have carried out field research—asked on the ground about salons, got actual customers' feedback, visited them myself, chatted with their staff—I most likely would have a very different perception than that which I got from online. Several years ago, before the world of digital, that is what I would have done. Word of mouth went a long way.

But now, instead of that, it is much easier to check businesses out online. See what they are up to, see how proactive they are, see what knowledge they have. And that is why it is so important to give off the right impression.

If you are currently happy with the amount of business you have and are not particularly bothered about taking a giant leap forward or really taking your business up to the next level, then it will not matter so much. You do not need to impress anyone; you're doing OK, and will probably continue to do so. However, you must not become too complacent. You may have a steady stream of business now, but as your competitors continue to develop their strategies online and strengthen their social media presence, your business could start to suffer. It might be worth following my advice, even if you are happy with where you are now. However, if you are not happy with where you are now and know deep down that your business could be so much more and be doing so much better, take stock of the examples I have given so far and start putting them into practice.

In today's world, we must be open minded and realize that the way we always did things is not how things are done now. A lot has changed and is still changing—how people shop, communicate, play games, get enjoyment, are very different and much of it has moved online. For those companies whose businesses are solely online, you are in a strong position. For those of you who are still getting to grips with email, you need to accept that you or someone designated by you must tackle the online world. Without it, your business will not flourish or grow.

You should have a digital strategy. Once you get the hang of it, you will wonder why it scared you so much in the first place. It is all about perception.

A few years back, a company I had worked for began posting content regularly. This was out of the blue; they had been very quiet for a while. But now it seemed, they were everywhere. Facebook, LinkedIn, Twitter, YouTube. Press releases about how well they were doing, sharing great content, emails were coming through much more frequently, push notes started popping up on my phone. "What is going on here?" I thought to myself. "Have they come into a lucrative opportunity or a new partnership, maybe?" As it happened, one of my old colleagues who was still at that company messaged me a couple of weeks later, just to catch up. I took the opportunity to ask how things were going and congratulated them on how well the business seemed to be doing; they seemed to be flying. I received a good-humored response, saying things had never been worse. They were losing customers and losing revenue.

They had created a new strategy whereby they were doing aggressive marketing campaigns to combat the downturn they were experiencing.

As it turned out, it worked. Many companies approached them with partnership opportunities, which worked out in their favour. Their sales increased because their target market saw all the hype and did not want to miss out, so they started to make purchases again!

PERCEPTION. It is all about how you portray yourself in the market!

What we have discussed so far concerning market segmentation and customer marketing is not time specific. I mean that the information is applicable, whether it was twenty years ago or twenty years into the future. However, when it comes to the tools used, these can change over time and when new tools or platforms emerge in the future, these same philosophies must be applied.

You can always refer to the "best practices" of a tool to get good guidance. I have much experience with numerous marketing tools and platforms and have had many successful campaigns generating high revenue returns and excellent results. This is what I am basing my information on. You can use many different channels to get your message out there, and each company's strategy will differ. If you have different products on offer, you should have a separate strategy for each one, which could mean adverts running on different platforms. But let us start with one of the most important marketing tools.

Website

[7]*According to the eCommerce Foundation, 88% of consumers will research product information before they make a purchase online or in the store.*

Before you initiate any form of advertising or promotions, the first port of call is making sure your website is up to scratch. Imagine seeing attractive professional looking adverts for a new paint shop, you see them online, you see them in the local paper, you hear them on the radio, and you think, "These guys seem to know what they are doing; I'll give them a shot." You call into the shop with high

---

[7]

expectations. However, the shop is very disorganized, not very neat or tidy, staff running around everywhere, different types of signs all over the place, shelves are messy, and you cannot seem to find anything you are looking for.

What would you do? I would likely leave. And that's probably what people will do if they come to your website after clicking on an advert and see a poorly put together site. Many clients have said to me, "Ah, the website isn't really important to us; we don't get business from it." And, oh, how right they are. I am not surprised they do not get business from it. It instills no confidence in anyone.

Having a modern, up-to-date, easy to follow website can add massive value to your company and gain you a huge amount of business that you did not know existed.

If you think you are fine without one, be content in the knowledge that not only are you losing out on sales, but you are losing out on potential business partnerships or opportunities. You could have a large business looking to secure a partner for a lucrative deal, and you will most likely be passed straight over if you do not have a decent website presence. It is time to get your website sorted.

You can get a website done for a lot less than you may think. Shop around, do some research. Maybe hire a freelancer. But it is crucial that you do get it sorted, one way or another. Your website must appeal to your target audience. Many companies believe their websites are very informative and easy for potential customers to understand. However, remember that while you know your business inside out, that does not mean your target audience will. I have lost count of the number of websites I have viewed, and after several minutes of browsing, I am none the wiser as to what the company sells.

Try it now. Look at your website and pretend that you are someone who knows nothing or very little about your company or industry or the products you sell. Really put yourself in their mind.

At first glance, can you easily tell what your company sells? Can you tell what the company stands for? What is it about? If you can, great. You are on the right track. But I am pretty sure many of you may be scratching your head. KEEP IT SIMPLE. And in language the audience understands.

Make sure it is obvious what your company provides. Do not overload people with too much information. A couple of sentences that describe exactly what you do should be near the top of the page. Keep your website fresh with the content you are sharing— update your news sections regularly with videos, articles, press releases, or whitepapers. And try to include as many videos as you can.

[8] *A study for Forbes in 2018 found that the average user spends 88% more time on a website with video.*

This can be easily done in-house through a good content management system, my preference being WordPress. Failing that, your go-to website person will add them and help you create the site your company deserves.

It is a great benefit if you can control your website internally. There are no delays when you need to change a price or product description, and you can upload news stories and photos very quickly. If you need an immediate response to something in the market, it can be done straight away. However, when you depend on someone outside the company, let us say a freelancer or a website company you have contracted, this can sometimes lead to frustrations if nobody is answering your calls or emails. People are in meetings, dealing with other clients, or at events all day. Having control internally would be much more beneficial for you and your company.

It is not difficult to manage. Just make sure whoever has built your site gives you access to the content management system. If there is

---

[8]

none with it, ask your website company to create one. A content management system is a tool used to manage your website. Controlling the website internally saves time; it is much more efficient and cost-effective. You can still get the web company to carry out the big stuff but if it is just images, text, and news stories that need changing and updating, manage it yourself internally.

There are numerous different software's, but personally, I prefer WordPress which is easy to use and very adaptable.

If you can use Microsoft Word and post a photo on Facebook, you can use a content management system. If you cannot, nominate someone in the office to familiarize themselves with it or else, outsource the work to whoever manages your website. But certainly, explore the option of taking the management in-house and do it if you can.

Some tips for creating a top-performing website.

Four Main Components of a Good Website:

1. *Architecture:* How the website it created – What Content Management System is used – What Plugins – Type of Backend System
2. *UX* (the experience): How easy it will be for the user. Interaction Design – Wireframes – Sitemap – Ease of Use – Navigation
3. *UI* (the medium): What the overall look will be. Visual Design – Colours – Branding – Links – Call to Actions
4. *Display:* The type of imagery you decide to use. Graphics and Text Formatting

- ➤ Information should be readily available.
- ➤ Visitors should not have to search the site to find something.

<u>The benefits of implementing best practices</u>

a) Increase User's Time on the site
b) Provides a better user experience
c) Leads to more return visits
d) Increase lead generation
e) Increase sales

➤ Make sure information is organized in a way that makes sense.
➤ Allow the user to navigate easily.
➤ Make the content easier to understand

This is just a quick list for you to use and help you understand how websites should be structured. Have a look at your current website and see how it rates in comparison to the above guidelines.

SEO

Search Engine Optimization is an essential part of your website. There is a lot involved in creating a good SEO strategy, so I will explain the basics. When writing text for your website, make sure to include highly ranked keywords—the words people would use to search for your website.

So, if it was a hair salon, keywords would be "hairdressers", "hair styling", "up styles", "blow-dry", "hair salons", etc. If it was a car dealership, "new cars", "used cars", "Ford cars", "Nissan cars", "vans", etc. would be useful. If you search on Google, you can usually find out what the main keywords are for your industry.

But common sense can go a long way, too. You know what your business is about, you know what the main keywords would be but make sure you also think of the consumer. What would someone looking for the products you sell type into a Google search? Write down ten to fifteen keywords that would be associated with your business. Now, when you are writing content for the website, make sure your content includes these keywords. This way, your page will be ranked higher by Google. Google change their rules a lot when it comes to SEO, so whatever the rules are now when I am writing this, they may have changed a little by the time you read this.

But whoever is building your website will be able to advise you. You should certainly get an SEO audit done by a freelancer and work on their recommendations. It is important to get an SEO audit to ensure that your website is user friendly, the site speed is up to scratch, and it has no error pages or issues.

These will show you how your current keywords are ranking or performing, and if you need to add more. Ask your current web company to carry one out for you but make sure you do it. If you are going to make all the changes needed and if you are going to make an effort to create an efficient and effective marketing strategy that delivers results, then you need to make sure you are ready for that business when it comes in. Some other factors to consider when it comes to SEO:

- ➤ **Highly ranked keywords** – When a user searches for the particular keyword
- ➤ **Optimised Pages** – By optimizing your content for one specific keyword, you tell the search engines what the page is about and what it should rank for.
- ➤ **Site Speed** – Slow loading sites provide bad user experience. Search engines know that people want to find answers as fast as possible, so they prefer to show sites that will load quickly for users. Load speed is a ranking factor.
- ➤ **Site Security** – Site security refers to the use of HTTPS encryption. Sites with HTTPS encryption have SSL certificates

that create a secure connection between a website and its users
- ➢ **Mobile Friendliness**
- ➢ **Site crawlability** - Crawlability allows search engines to scan a website and review its content, so they can determine what the page is about and how it should rank.
- ➢ **Quality Content** - Content is one of the most important SEO ranking factors. Search engines want to provide the best results possible, so they give top rankings to sites that have well-researched, in-depth, and well-crafted content.

If you are spending budget on advertising campaigns, content creation, etc. you must ensure that there is an efficient website to deal with it otherwise not only could you be losing business, but you will create a negative experience and that potential customer or client may never come back.

Google Analytics

This is a convenient tool for showing you statistics about people's behaviour when they come to your site. It will show you how many visitors a day, where they are from, how they got there (whether they searched for you on Google or came from another website). It tells what keywords people used to find you. It shows how long people spend on each page. It shows the most popular content on your website.

It can be very beneficial for identifying areas of your website that receive little or no engagement. By doing so you can replace that section with something else and see if performance improves. If you have an e-commerce website, it is an excellent tool to show you how to improve your sales. For example, if you seem to be getting a lot of traffic to your website but are not getting any online orders, google analytics can be great for looking into the detail. It can show you exactly where a site visitor leaves your page. They may have added products to the cart, as if they are about to purchase, but not gone through with it.

And Google Analytics can show on what page you are losing people. Why would people be dropping off when they have added an item to the cart? This allows you to investigate it yourself or get your web team to do so. It could be that your delivery fee is too high, or maybe it gets complicated and confusing at the checkout. Maybe it is not user friendly enough. But this allows you to change things around and see if making changes will show a difference in sales. You could be having people landing on the home page, going to the product page, and dropping off there. Wherever you see the drop-off, there may be an issue. It could be that there are too many steps to purchase a product. This can happen.

People become frustrated if they keep being taken to another page and another page.

Once they can see the product and the product details, there should be a button where they can just click "add to cart" and they can check out straight away. Cut down the steps in the process to purchase; make it as quick and simple as you can. Go through it as if you are someone who knows nothing about your product or business. Remember, because you are familiar with it, you will believe that it is an easy process. So ask your friends and family to go through the purchasing process and get their feedback on where they think you could make improvements. If you make changes but are still not seeing any results, it might be worth looking at getting an online chat option.

This is relatively easy to set up and it can be managed by someone in the office. It means that if someone is not 100% convinced to purchase yet, they can type a quick message to one of your staff and get an answer straight away. This will give them the confidence to make the purchase.

You will need to put the resources in place so this can happen but it will be worth it. I have had experiences where putting an online chat option has greatly increased online sales.

Before I finish on websites, please do not have a pop-up box flash up in people's faces the second they land on your site. Many people click straight off the site when this happens. Of course, there is nothing wrong with having a pop-up box on your website but people must have a chance to have a look around first. If a potential customer does not know exactly what your company offers and at what prices, throwing a promo box up straight away to sign up for a newsletter will be very annoying. This mustn't happen for at least ten to fifteen seconds otherwise you will lose visitors and therefore lose possible sales.

However, it is a good idea to have a sign-up box and encourage people to register for your newsletter—it just needs to be done in the right way.

[9]*Sumo, a leading provider of pop-up software, researched over 2 billion pop-ups. "If they haven't read two words on your site, then how can you expect them to subscribe/buy/do anything for you? Only 8% had pop-ups appear in the 0-4 second mark. And guess what the lowest-converting pages had in common? Rushed pop-ups."*

This research reinstates the importance of getting the timing right for your pop-ups.

9

Chapter Five –Marketing Tools – Social Media

Facebook

[10]*Facebook continues to grow every year since it launched in 2004, in both active users and time spent on the platform. It is still the most used social platform, with nearly 2.45 billion monthly active users.* It is important to post regularly on Facebook, every three to four days, ideally. Even daily in some cases. It could be several times of the day. Every company is different. But if you do not currently have a strategy in place, it is better to start slowly and build on it. Your posts do not always have to be company related.

They could be about the weather, something funny, or some industry news. While you want to be posting quality content, you do not want to be just selling or talking about your products constantly. Mix it up a bit. Ideally, you should put a calendar in place, so you know what days you need to post and what type of material. Do this at the start of each month and it will be a great help to you.

If advertising directly to consumers, you can create very targeted campaigns. For example, imagine I want to advertise a used car, let us say a Volkswagen Golf, in excellent condition.

I know from research that young guys between the age of twenty and thirty are most likely to purchase it; I can create an advert that will appeal to that audience and make sure only they see the advert. This cuts down on cost and increases your click-through rate as you show adverts relevant to that audience.

10

[11]*As Jay Baer once stated, "If content is fire, social media is gasoline."*

We will speak about Facebook several times throughout this book. Your company should have an active Facebook page, no matter what industry you are in or what markets you are targeting. For Business to Consumer, it can be an excellent tool for running promotions and winning you new customers at little cost. For Business to Business, it is a great tool to build your brand and overall market presence.

LinkedIn While there is certainly potential for Business to Consumer marketing on LinkedIn, Business to Business opportunities would be more prevalent. [12]*660 million users are on the professional network in more than 200 countries. The platform is also home to over 30 million companies. According to LinkedIn, their growth rate is at two new members joining per second. Among the 660 million LinkedIn members, Europe has over 206 million users. The United States has over 167 million, while the remaining members are from other countries and territories.*

Posting good content on your LinkedIn page regularly and then following it up with an advertising campaign is extremely effective. You can build campaigns that will only be shown to the actual people you want. For example, if I am a building contractor looking for large company projects, I can create adverts that will only reach the decision-makers. I can pick the actual companies by name and target the people working in those companies by job titles, such as project managers or procurement managers. This also allows you to put together an advert that you know they will be interested in.

11

12

I would highly recommend creating a LinkedIn Company page and posting content at least once a week. Regardless of whether you are Business to Business or Business to Consumer.

Twitter

Twitter very much focuses on hashtags – # – which are used when posting content. These are used to identify messages on a specific topic.

Most social media platforms tend to use them but especially Twitter and Instagram. My advice when creating hashtags is to start with SEO keywords, use popular hashtags, create branded hashtags, including your company name. Monitor your community's hashtags to see what is trending. You do not want to miss out on an opportunity if your whole community is tweeting about a certain topic that you could add quality information to. Do not add spaces/punctuation, or it will not be recognized. Avoid using lots of hashtags and keep them short.

Twitter is a great tool for raising an individual's profile as well as the company itself. Choose someone to be the face of your company, for example, the managing director, the head of sales or operations or maybe the marketing manager.

Have them create videos and do talks and presentations at events, all the time, tweeting their knowledge and content. This is a great way of building confidence and credibility in your brand. Ideally, the MD/owner should do it but if you are not comfortable, assign someone with good knowledge and ask them to take it on as part of their job. Get them to review products while videoing themselves or get them to talk about some latest news in your industry and give their opinion. Whatever it might be, get them out there and get them to tweet what they are involved in continuously, very much building your brand.

[13]*Twitter is the preferred social network for news consumption. 85% of small and medium business users use Twitter to provide customer service. 34% of Twitter users are females, and 66% are males.*

These statistics from Twitter are according to Salman Aslam, Founder and CEO of Omnicore, a leading Healthcare Digital Advertising and Marketing Agency.

A large number of businesses are already using Twitter to handle customer service. It is worth looking into if you have not already. I have used it for posting content and advertising, and it is very user friendly, like most of the platforms out there. The stats show that 66% of the users are male. Keep that in mind, also. It is an interesting fact and should help you decide how much resources you should invest in the platform considering your audience and potential market.

Instagram

Instagram is an excellent platform for showcasing products and services.[14] *In 2019, the percentage of US adults who use Instagram rose from 35% to 37%, and the active reported users have held steady at around 1 billion people.*

This is good for getting attractive videos and images out there. Make sure to use crisp, clear, professional-looking content. And make it interesting. Rather than just posting a picture of a product, place it somewhere of interest. Perhaps have someone trying it out or do something with it to make it more interesting. It is an extremely beneficial platform for the beauty industry, such as make-up, hair styling, tans, creams, lotions, and skincare. It is also powerful in the travel and food sectors as these types of images are

---

13

14

appealing to most people. We all want to look good, eat good food and go on holiday!

If you do not already utilize Instagram, have a look at what your competitors are doing. Or even look at the larger companies in your industry and take some inspiration from them. It will give you an idea of what type of strategy to create—no point in reinventing the wheel. Of course, that does not mean you copy exactly what they are doing but it will give you the right idea and put you on the right track to create an appropriate concept for the platform.

Instagram also has a straightforward advertising platform similar to Facebook. In fact, when running adverts on Facebook, you can choose to include them on Instagram, cutting out a lot of work. In March 2012, Facebook bought Instagram for $1 billion! Wow.

Their platforms are linked when it comes to posting and running campaigns, which is convenient. You do not even have to have an Instagram account to run adverts on the platform; your Facebook account will run them for you. Hashtags are very important on Instagram as with Twitter, so make sure to get three or four in each time you post.

[15]*Kim Garst*, an international author and one of the world's most retweeted people among digital marketeers, says, "Sell-sell-sell sales methods simply do not work on social media."

Make sure you mix up your content on all platforms.

YouTube Channel

A YouTube channel for your videos would be very beneficial. It is an excellent form of digital marketing and really raises your presence in the digital world. It will help you get noticed by the right people and may even create some lucrative opportunities for you and the company. You can run ad campaigns on the YouTube platform, too.

15

So, if you find one of your videos is getting a lot of engagement, put a bit of budget behind it, and it will really take off! Google owns YouTube, so you can use your Google ad account to run ad campaigns on its platform. YouTube has two billion monthly active users. [16]*A 2019 study by the Pew Research Center found that YouTube users outnumber those of any other platform in the US, with 73% of US adults identifying as users. Only Facebook, at 69%, comes anywhere near.*

This just shows you how many people you could reach. I know this is USA based, but it is used all over the world. It is probably safe to say that most of your target audience is on YouTube. Some are on it and do not realize it – like my mother. She tends to click on a video she might see on Facebook, which lands her on YouTube, and then another video comes up that she is interested in, and she will start watching that one and so on. She has no idea that she is actually on a platform called YouTube; she still thinks she is on Facebook. But you can place your content in front of her, as YouTube know what content she likes to watch, and so she will likely see your advert if she is within your target audience. Video is the way forward. I know I have mentioned it a lot, but I cannot stress how important it is to your marketing strategy, especially when you already have the goods. You have the knowledge. Get it out there!

Social media is such an important part of your Marketing Strategy. However, it can be time consuming and for this reason a lot of companies do not keep on top if it. I highly recommend that if you do not have a marketing resource in-house, you hire a social media company or freelancer to manage this for you. It is a vital part of the journey to becoming a market leader!

16

Chapter Six – Direct Marketing

Email Campaigns

This is one of my favourite tools. Email campaigns are extremely beneficial; they can be very targeted and reveal vast information about your audience.[17]*According to a survey carried out by Adobe, which looked at how consumers communicate across email and other channels, time spent checking personal email is up 17%year-over-year. Consumers are checking personal email an average of 2.5 hours on a typical weekday. They also spend an average of 3.1 hours, checking work email.* As you can see, email is an essential part of your marketing strategy.

How often you send emails to your customer base will depend on the type of industry you are in and whether it is Business to Business or Business to Consumer.

For B to B, I would recommend once a week; maybe every two weeks, depending on what you sell or do. For B to C, it depends on how many products you sell but probably twice a week would be enough. Emailing people every day can be too much for people. But whatever you decide to do, be consistent. If you decide that you will send out emails to your customer base every Tuesday afternoon, then send them at the same time every week. That way, customers will come to expect them which can be a good thing. Before you come up with any content on what you want to send out, SEGMENT your database. This can be quite time-consuming, but once it is done, all you have to do is add to it in the future. Pick at least three sub-

---

[17]

segments and separate people into the three groups (as mentioned earlier in the book). This will mean that every week you will be sending three different emails using images and content that would suit each segment.

The real beauty of email marketing is the analytics you receive. There are lots of different email software's you can use, some for free if you only have a small number of email addresses. I have always used Mailchimp and find it very easy to navigate. But most of the softwares are similar and are very user friendly. Do a bit of research and see which one you believe would suit you the most.

After you send out your email campaign, you can review reports and find out who opened it, who clicked on what article, how many times they opened it and if they forwarded it to anyone else. This is very beneficial for Business-to-Business companies as you can create leads from the analytics.

For example, imagine I provide software for Smart TVs, and I can see from the reports that Bob from Sharp TV has opened my email. In fact, I can see that he has opened it several times and clicked on one of the articles featuring our latest product six times. Now I know that Bob is very interested in that product.

However, you must be careful how you go about this. You should not ring Bob, let him know how many times he looked at the email and ask him to place an order. This would be extremely annoying, and he probably will never open another email from your company again. While it is perfectly legal to see this information, it is not really something we can comfortably approach people about. It is better to find a more subtle way. Chances are if Bob is interested in the email, he will give you a call himself.

However, if you hear nothing after four or five days, you could always call Bob or drop him an email asking him how things were and that you were just touching base. Sneaky? Maybe. But if it gets you a big order? Happy days. And the beauty of email is you could have many people interested from just one email. That is a lot of following up to do from which at least one order will hopefully come. This is an order you might not have got had you not, firstly, sent a targeted email with relevant information, and secondly, been able to see who opened it which prompted you to touch base and succeed in getting the order.

Email marketing can be extremely effective for Business-to-Business companies—especially those with very high investment products or services. I used to use it regularly in many companies where I worked. I would study who was opening it, what they were reading, and how often they opened it. Then I would create a list of leads and send them on to the relevant sales reps to follow up.

Email can also be great for Business to Consumer, but more in a promotional way. It is not recommended to just send sales emails to customers. A variety of company stories, competitions, latest promotions, new products, etc., will keep them interested. Then study the reports and find out which parts of the emails get attention and what parts were ignored. If you try a particular section every week, see whether it gets any clicks, then you know if your audience is interested in this content. Relevant changes can be made from there.

Marketing tactics are very much about trial and error. What works for one company may not work for another. Facebook could be great for one company, but LinkedIn does not benefit them. Then you have someone else who relies on LinkedIn totally and have no Facebook presence. It is all about trial and error and finding out what works for you. Do not rule out anything until you have tested it. You should have a presence on both platforms and adopt appropriate strategies.

What you post on LinkedIn and what you post on Facebook will be very different. For B to B, it can help raise a company's profile in the community by being on Facebook and posting company updates, staff pictures, events, competitions, etc. And for B to C, being on

LinkedIn could provide you with partnership opportunities you never thought existed.

Emails should be sent out at appropriate times. If you send them to more than one country, be sure that they are time zone sensitive. Noon can be a good time. This way, you are reaching those who check their mail at lunchtime and in the evening. Research into what time and what days are most effective can be useful as these trends tend to change. As I am writing this now, Tuesday is the most effective day; in other words, emails get the highest amount of opens as an average across all industries. It is unlikely, but that could have changed by the time you are reading this. Also, every audience is different. Carry out a couple of test campaigns. Split your database into two. And send half on Tuesday and half on Wednesday and see which gets the most open rates.

You can test lots of things by doing this. It is called a split test option. You can send out the same email but use two or three different subject lines. The email will only be sent to 10% of your database; then, it will automatically send the email which received the most opens to the remaining 90%. You can set the testing time. You can schedule them for an hour, three hours, twenty-four hours, whatever you like. But it is best to give it a few hours at least to get a good response rate to go on.

It is very straight forward to do. This is an excellent way to really get the most out of your email campaigns.

It is important to get the timings right, especially if you have a business with no online ordering system. I have often received emails after business hours which I was interested in. I may have wanted to make a purchase or just find out more about it but when I call the company, they are closed until the next day. Of course, I could call the next morning. However, it is likely I will forget to call or may not feel the same need for the product as the night before. This will result in the company losing out on a sale due to the time they sent the email. How many other potential customers did this happen to? Timing is critical. Get it right.

[18]*Below is a graph generated by research carried out by Technology Advice.*

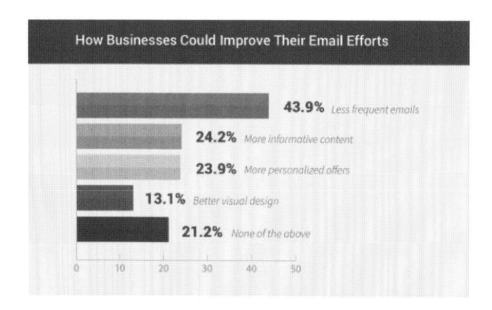

TechnologyAdvice – Research Result Table

It shows what people said when asked how businesses could improve emails. 44% said that businesses could improve their email efforts by sending less frequent emails! 24% said more personalized content would be better and 24% said they wanted more relevant content.

Both personalized and relevant content fall into the market segmentation, target marketing approach.

18

Blog

In addition to updating the news sections on your website with stories and content, if you really want to become a content king (or queen), it is a good idea to start a blog. A blog differs from the news section in that it is a more personal opinion on topics, and it provides the option of allowing people to engage through comments and sharing.

If you are very knowledgeable about your industry or someone in your company is, it would be really useful to create a blog. Write personal opinions about topics in your industry, be open to people commenting on what you say and be ready to comment back to any questions asked. It is great exposure, and if it goes viral, you can generate considerable coverage within the industry. And it is free— apart from your time, of course! Start with one every week or two and if it is well received, you can do it more frequently. Blogs are also an excellent tool for improving your SEO strategy.

Push Notes – If you have an App

A push note is a simple text message that allows marketers to reach mobile users at any time. As the message pops up in front of you, the open rate is usually much higher than targeted messaging.[19]*According to **Segmentify**, research indicates the open rates for push note messages are as much as 50% higher than email*, which demonstrates how powerful they can be. However, they are only effective when used correctly.

Have you ever heard a notification ping on your phone at 2 a.m., waking you from a magnificent dream to find a message from some game you downloaded to tell you that you have unlocked a new gift?

---

[19]

Or that your carrots are ready to be picked? Or that the mayor of the town has invited you to a party? Or something even more annoying? I have—many, many times— which is why I immediately turn off the push notes related to whatever app has annoyed me. ALWAYS take note when scheduling a push note campaign, that there are multiple time zones and research the best times to send push notes within your industry.

You must ensure you are not sending messages to people in the middle of the night. To be able to send a message directly to one of your target audience, or one of your customers, and have it appear right in front of them on their phone, which you know they will read, is a hugely powerful marketing tool. Do not lose your opportunity by sending messages at the wrong time. Push notes have unbelievable capabilities—such a powerful tool if used correctly.

Have you ever received a push note or an email telling you about a great promotion that you are really interested in? But when you click on it, there is no mention anywhere of this promotion. This shows a huge lack of communication within the company and it can be damaging as your audience will stop clicking on your promotions if you are not consistent with the offerings. Whatever it was that made the person click on the link, they will want to see that same information wherever they land on your site.

Inn-App messaging – if app related

In-App messaging can be very effective if you have a game or an app that offers purchases within it. In-App messages are messages delivered to your users while they are directly active in your mobile app.[20] *In fact, according to Airship, a leading customer engagement platform, a Mobile Engagement Benchmark Survey found that In-App messaging typically receives 8x the direct response rates of push*

20

notifications. In combination with push notifications, In-App messages receive an average engagement rate of 26% for a medium-performing app. High-performing apps receive a read rate of 44%, so the opportunity for engagement through In-App messages is high.

This demonstrates the importance of utilizing this tool. You can track the user's journey every time they open your app so you can have different messages for different users. For example, if you have someone who has not opened the app for a while, it would be nice to have a "Welcome back, Bob" message for them the next time they do open it. Then you could offer them a special promo: "As we haven't seen you in a while, we are going to give you 10% off today". That is a nice touch; Bob will appreciate it and feel good. However, if someone comes back daily, you could say, "Hi, Bob. Happy Tuesday! Receive 10 free credits if you make a purchase today!" I am not suggesting giving him something daily—just every now and then. This will also make Bob happy. If he is a daily user, he is getting added value as he would most likely be purchasing anyway, but this is likely to cement the purchase.

Anyone who has any type of games app should really be utilizing In-App and push note messaging and have numerous different segments and associated messaging with each segment. The more targeted and segmented, the higher the return. There is huge potential to grow your revenues through this form of marketing, considering these people are already your customers. And it is so much easier to sell to an existing customer than try to gain a new one.

Cross Marketing

It is widely known that it is much easier to sell a new product to an existing customer than a new one. [21]*According to OutboundEngine, an online marketing software company, acquiring a new customer can cost five times more than retaining an existing customer.* Your existing customer base already trusts you and tend to be loyal. When you bring out something new, and it relates to them, they will likely want to buy it. However, it is important how this message is communicated. Inundating your existing customers with news about this product is not going to be helpful. Continue to carry out your regularly targeted campaigns, but always include a section about this product in the email. It is alright to send one message to your existing base wholly about your new product or service when you first launch as you are just letting them know about it. But after that, leave it as a small addition to your existing campaigns. Your customers are your customers because they have been buying a certain product/service from you. I do not recommend potentially annoying them by continually trying to sell them something else.

For example, every week I send my poker newsletters to the poker audiences; this can be made up of multiple stories. Though the headline will always be poker related, the other sections can promote slots, roulette, or tournaments. Or, if I have a software business, the main headline story will be about something related to the target audience, but in the other sections, there is information about other products. Encourage people to sign up for a newsletter specifically for updates on that actual product. Then you are growing your audience for the new or other products you have.

21

In addition, when a customer makes a purchase, you can offer them a discount on your other products as a result. You see this regularly with companies. For example, most recycling companies will give you a discount on skip hire if you are a household customer. Offering discounts on other products or services that you have is a great way of cross marketing as you are not forcing it on people. The offer is there, and they know it. They might not need a skip today, but when they do, they will remember the discount offer. Making them aware the offers are there is beneficial as when the time comes, they will likely remember and make the purchase with you.

Webinars

Webinars are an excellent source of lead generation and are also a great tool for building relationships with existing customers. While they can be used for Business to Consumer, they are much more popular in the Business-to-Business world, especially in a market where the product or service may be a bit technical. Holding education webinars every week is a great way of building a connection with current and potential clients. Ensure that whatever you intend to broadcast will be of help to those who will be watching. You are essentially giving something away for nothing but with the view that the current client will continue to buy your products and that your potential client will come to you when it is time for them to purchase what you sell. Think about the different topics within your industry. Think of the different issues or problems that people seem to come across a lot. Set out a webinar schedule for every quarter and once you have outlined the topics and what content you will be discussing, start to market this schedule.

Share the information in your email campaigns and social media platforms. Make sure you use a good webinar software like GoToMeeting, for example. Set up each webinar in the software before you start to advertise them.

By doing this, people can register well in advance and will receive reminders about it. Creating a schedule at the start of each quarter means you are organized and know what is coming. [22]*"About 29% of your attendees won't register for your presentation until the day of the event itself. However, webinar statistics also show that 17% of your attendees will probably sign up more than 15 days before the big day."* That is, according to Medium.com, the knowledge platform.

Get your staff involved; they can regularly let your current and potential customers know of the upcoming webinars. By constantly communicating the fact you are holding these webinars, the spaces should fill up quite quickly. You can so these yourself or simply create a presentation and speak to people about it. Don't worry about running out of ideas as every time you hold a webinar, you will get more and more questions from customers and some of these questions will actually need their own webinar to answer. More ideas for webinars will flow from the ones you start with—that is why I recommend doing them by quarter. They are a great tool, especially in a Business-to-Business environment. They can also be good for a sales team. For example, if a sales rep is trying to close a sale, but the client is a bit unsure as he is not fully convinced of how your product works, you can direct them to a webinar about that exact topic the next week and send them the link. This gives the client a sense of security, and once they attend the webinar, I am sure the deal will be closed as any concerns they may have had should be put to bed.

Effectively you are removing the barriers to sale. These webinars are a great way of helping the sales team to secure new clients.

22

Create a folder of content that you can utilise on an ongoing basis and add quality materials to it. Here are some forms of content that you can create multiple formats;

Video Creation
This is a hugely effective form of marketing and it costs nothing but time to do.
[23]*Studies show that 54% of consumers want to see more video content from a brand or business they support (HubSpot, 2018).*
Choose a topic every month and create three or four videos around it. Get someone to record you with your phone or just record yourself if you feel more comfortable. It does not have to be you. It can be someone within the company who is knowledgeable enough. All it involves is speaking for a minute or maybe two, doing a demo on one of your products, giving some tips on an item that not everyone is aware of, or giving your opinion on something happening in the industry. Capture stock being offloaded, shelves being stacked, a truck being unloaded, software being developed, whatever it may be. For example, I once recorded a video of a crane taking wood pellets of a ship, put it on Facebook, and got thousands of views within two days. It was a surprise but clearly the interest was there.
Do not underestimate yourself or the information you possess. People much prefer to gain information from a video than having to

---

23

read it. [24]*Based on the 2018 State of Social Video Marketer Trends report, 73% of consumers claim that they have been influenced by a brand's social media presence when making a purchasing decision.*

Start creating videos and share them on your social media platforms and website. They are an excellent marketing tool and really build the credibility of your brand. What you **think** and what **is** can be very different. You may feel no one will be interested in a video of you offloading stock, washing vehicles, maybe revamping a store or developing new software, but people love watching videos of behind the scenes. So, capture it on your phone and share it. It can be very powerful. And it will not cost you anything other than time.

[25] *A survey conducted by Wyzowl shows that nearly eight out of every ten users have purchased a piece of software or app after watching the brand's video.*

Press Releases

Press releases, in my experience, are one of the drivers behind perception. And perception is key. Press releases sound very professional, and when they are released in the market, they give off the perception of "They are issuing a press release now; they must be doing really well." Anyone can issue a press release. If you really want your company to start being taking seriously as a key player in the industry, start coming up with some ideas. What is a press release, really? It is simply information about your company. It could be anything. It could be a new employee that has joined your team, it could be about how the weather is affecting your business, or it could be about the latest financial results.

The very bottom line is that it does not matter all that much. Unless it is something huge that people find very interesting, then

---

24

25

most people will just glance over the content it contains. But what will stick in their mind is the fact that you RELEASED a story. You have been noticed. You are on people's radars. You have gone up in people's opinions. The PERCEPTION of your business is beginning to, just a tiny bit, change. Because releasing one press release is not going to do anything. But it will get the ball rolling, the heads will turn, and interest will peak, which is exactly what you want.

Aim to do a release every four to six weeks. You can write up a page on whatever you have decided you want to share with people. Try to think of something that people would find interesting and might want to share or comment on. I know I said it does not essentially matter what you put in it, but you want to start on the right foot if this is a new strategy.

And while perception is key, getting it right from the start is too. Once you are up and running with a good marketing strategy and have releases going out regularly, the content will no longer be as important. But you are at the beginning (for this example) of your Strategic Marketing Plan, and therefore first impressions are crucial. Think of something people in your industry might find interesting about your company. Or if you have recently done a deal with another company, or won a contract, ask that company if you can write a joint release. Do not underestimate yourself or your business. Don't dismiss things and believe people wouldn't be interested in it, if it is good, genuine information, put it in a release.

There are many PR distribution companies who will get your release out to the media and the community. They can vary very much in price. I would take two approaches. The first option is the more expensive one and the better one to start with. PR distribution companies will have different channels for sharing releases. The more expensive ones can usually get you featured in all the media you require, local, national, or global. In this way, you can guarantee coverage, and you will begin to get noticed. Paying for the first three or four releases would be a good move, perhaps getting a deal for a package as it will take a good six to twelve months to get your company in the position you want it to be in. The second option is to use a much less expensive company. They will get your release out, but most likely to a lot less credible media channels or much smaller ones. However, this can be good to use when you have become a market leader, and you want to let the market know you are ahead of the curve. Unless it is something important that you want the world to know, after establishing yourself as a leader, you can use the cheaper option now and then.

Press Releases are also great from an SEO perspective as your article will be all over the internet and it will come up in searches if you have good keywords in the content. After that, you can mix it up a bit: small news stories, release internally or with a small PR distribution agency; large ones, pay to distribute. Please remember that I am giving you advice based on my experience. Do some research if you want to look at some other ways to get them out [26] *B2B Press, a top PR company, says that, "Press releases increase the visibility of your brand in the media. Press releases enable you to be perceived as an expert in your industry."* So, get your thinking caps on!

Whitepapers

Whitepapers are an excellent way of raising your company profile as a professional. Again, it is all about perception here. A whitepaper is meant to help readers understand an issue or solve a problem they may have. It is usually six to eight pages and includes information about a specific topic that might be complex or difficult to understand. Now this will not apply to all businesses, obviously, but it is particularly applicable to software, technology, and financial companies. If you or someone in your company has a lot of

---

26

knowledge about what you do, get them to start using that information to create whitepapers. Research the best way to go about writing one.

However, if you have the knowledge, you should absolutely be using it. You can post these on social media platforms, particularly LinkedIn, and in time, if you are posting useful videos, articles, and whitepapers, people may start going to your website when they need to find a solution for an issue they have. That is when you become a market leader—when it is your company that people think of when they stumble upon a problem or an issue that they cannot resolve independently. Think about a company that is always posting content, good content. Are they seen as a market leader? They likely are, or they are on their way to being one.

It is not just large companies that can post regularly on social media. There is no reason you cannot, no matter how small you are. Regularly post solid information from your industry that is helpful through articles, videos, whitepapers, news stories or whatever format you choose. If people see frequent posts from you with quality content, you will go massively up in their opinions and be on their radar. It is not going to happen overnight. You need to keep this going and build momentum. PLEASE do not stop after a few months because you feel you are not getting anything back. YOU ARE! You just have not seen it yet.

You are building your brand and credibility. It takes time. I have often seen companies sharing great content and receiving high engagement levels in response to what they are doing. Then suddenly, after a few months, it just stops. Perhaps the marketing person has left and was not replaced. It could be that whoever was doing it hasn't the time anymore; maybe they felt they were not getting a return. I do not know the reason.

However, what I do know is that it reflects badly on the company when this happens. What do your audience think? How does it affect your community? Someone may think of your brand, realize they haven't seen you on social media in a while and wonder whether you are still in business. They may check your Facebook page and see there has been no activity in a few months. If you are lucky, they will call you or check your website but they may check out other companies if they feel you are no longer in business. Some will be wondering why you have stopped posting on social media; they might believe something is wrong or the company is no longer doing very well. People may think something negative has happened.

SO, KEEP AT IT. Be patient. It takes time to build your credibility and trust amongst your audience. Do not give in because you feel you are not getting results; you never know who is watching your activity Perhaps you are hoping to be bought out—sharing great quality content will make you a much more attractive proposition to a company than a business who is silent. So, get your social media strategy in order and get posting!

Testimonials

Testimonials—or customer reviews—are an essential part of your business. More and more people look online to research something they are going to purchase. To gain some confidence in what we are about to buy, we feel more secure when reading positive reviews or testimonials from someone or a company highlighting the excellent experience they have had or how great the product is. It is an essential part of getting the sale.

[27] *"Testimonials affirm our credibility and trust. Nowadays, this is called social proof. "This is according to Vikram Rajana, Forbes Councils Member.*

Ask some of your customers for a testimonial. Better still, write something yourself, email it to them and ask if it is alright to put their name to it. This will be more convenient for the customer.

---

[27]

People often have no problem agreeing to a review or testimonial, but it can be difficult to get them to provide one as they are so busy. It may help to ask them first and then say, "If you want, I'll write out a couple of lines and send it to you. Just reply back if you're OK with it or want to change it in any way." That tends to be the quickest and most effective way. This way, you can mix it up a bit and ensure the comments aren't all the same.

Having a "partners we work with" section can also be beneficial. Your potential audience will feel much more secure when they see these highly credible logos on your site. Think of the companies you work with and ask if you can display their logo as a partner.

This goes for both Business to Consumer and Business to Business. While B to C will not likely phone the customer, it can be very beneficial to send out a follow-up email after receiving the product or experiencing the service.

Ask them for a review and even incentivize them to do one by creating a competition. For example: "Review our product and be in with a chance to win a weekend away." Their comments can help show any flaws the product might have and enable you to make improvements, and the positive reviews can be used on your website and marketing material.

Google Ads

Google Ads are an effective tool for creating and displaying online adverts. Google will target people when they are scrolling through the internet, when they are in certain apps, when they are watching videos, reading articles, etc. When your target audience is scrolling through their phones or computers, your advert pops up in front of them. You only show these adverts to those likely to be interested. By doing this, you are much less likely to annoy or frustrate the person and there is a good chance that they will click on your advert.

This is very helpful if you have a specific promotion or new product. It also raises awareness of your company if you are not widely known. It is a great tool for brand awareness and getting your name out there. It also helps with website rankings as it increases traffic and people spending time on your site. What has worked best, in my experience, is running a generic brand awareness campaign for a month or two to get your brand out there. It does not need to be a hard sell— just who you are and what you do. You will only appear for the keywords that apply to your business, so most people who see your advert will be within your target audience.

Then when this audience is familiar with seeing your advertisement, you can hit them with a promotion. Change the advert from a generic standard one, to a hard sell. For example, "20% off for one week only" or "€100 Discount Today". In my twenty years of working in marketing across different sectors, the money value always proved more successful than the percentage discounts.

In support of this, [28]*Agilence, a leading data analytics company, stated, "Psychologically, the consumer views the dollar-off promotion as the better deal, so the dollar-off promotion is more popular, drives more sales for the targeted item, and increases average basket size."*

However, you should try them both and see what works best for your business.

Retargeting

Retargeting is an option in Google Ads (many companies also provide this service) and is extremely effective.

Have you ever gone on a holiday site, browsing through packages, but then clicked off and forgot about it only to have adverts from the same holiday site keep appearing? Or maybe you were looking online at a new set of golf clubs and suddenly, everywhere you look is the set of golf clubs! Yes, this can be annoying, but once it is handled and carried out correctly, it is an extremely effective tool. Basically (very basically), a piece of code is placed on the backend of your website. It collects data when people arrive on your site. You can then choose to use this data to run ad campaigns targeted at those who have been on your website.

Don't bombard people with stuff but it is worth running two to three campaigns up to a week after they left your site. I would not recommend pursuing it much longer as you do not want a potential consumer to form a negative opinion of your company. You have given them a few chances to make the purchase but they have said no. Leave it at that and trust that when they are ready, they will come back.

28

Industry Websites

This would be geared more towards Business to Business. However, it could also benefit Business to Consumers. Most industries will have one, if not more, main industry website or magazine which provides all the up-to-date news, new technologies, the latest companies doing well, etc. You might sometimes see big write-ups on companies and interviews with the MDs or CEOs, and you might envy them. Well, that can be you. Most of these spreads are done at a cost. If you agree to take a page advert in their magazine they will often offer to do a write-up on your company as part of the deal. It is how they do business. This type of marketing is usually quite an investment, but there tends to be good negotiating room. You should certainly explore the option of doing one of these features at least once a year.

This is not a form of marketing that produces mass sales. It is a tool for building credibility toward your brand and could create lucrative opportunities. A company may be on the lookout for somebody just like you and your firm. Be in the right place at the right time, and your investment could prove substantial.

Awards

Awards are a great way of instilling credibility in your business and they are not too difficult to get. The big awards may be more difficult, but you should apply for them anyway. Apply for all the awards within your industry that are available to you. There is a good chance you will be shortlisted (usually a large number of companies are shortlisted) and then you can advertise the fact you were shortlisted for whatever award it was, even if you do not win.

Also, look into other, smaller, awards you may be able to pick up. Some of these may have an entry fee, but you will likely receive an award of some sort. You have to start somewhere and eventually you may start to pick up the big ones.

Believe in your company. After all, if you do not believe in it, how do you expect anyone else to? Everyone has a chance. Do it. Do not ponder on it. Just do it. All you have to do is fill out an application form, answer a few questions, and send it off! Bam. Done. Have you started yet?

Chapter Ten – Events

Events are usually quite costly affairs. It will depend on the size and budget you have in place as to how many you decide to attend and have a presence at. You may question whether they are worth it or not. If you have the budget to have a stand at events related to your industry, it is always good to be seen there. However, if you are budget conscious, you can still have a presence without having a stand by pursuing a speaking opportunity instead. There will always be a one-, two- or three-day seminar where industry experts give talks at these events. They are usually one-hour slots where someone gets up on stage and talks about a specific topic. Anyone can do this.

Usually, you can work out a deal with the organizers to secure a speaking slot if you agree to a small ad campaign in their brochure or a small advert on their website. It can be more beneficial to be up on stage than have a stand because the people who attend the event are usually your target audience and most of them will be watching the talks and panel discussions. During the seminar, when someone is giving a talk, they are very likely to check out the program to see who the person is and their background. Then during the breaks, they will visit the stands.

Consider this: what opinion do you form of the person and their company when you see them up on stage speaking? Would you consider them an expert? Would you be confident about buying one of their products or services? Do they instill confidence that they have a good product or service? I am sure they do. And that could easily be you up there. It is not difficult to get a speaking slot. Explore options to try and secure one rather than a stand or in addition to a stand. It can be nerve-wracking but if you choose a topic that you are passionate about, it will make it much easier. You will not have to remember what to say. Just get up and give the audience tips on what they should or shouldn't be doing and offer them good advice. People will want to hear what you have to say. Do not use it as a sales pitch. That is cringeworthy. I have seen many people do this, and the speed at which the audience switch off or even leave the room can be seconds. Speak about something that they will find interesting. If you offer good credible advice, people will be impressed; they will say to themselves or their colleague, "Who is this guy/girl?"

They will find out what company you are from, they will look at your website (your recently updated website!), and they will be even more impressed. This is what leads to opportunities that could prove very lucrative.

You are building your brand and building people's confidence in your company, and you will begin to be seen as an industry expert. When you are putting out good content regularly, speaking at events, being seen in industry magazines, you are massively raising your profile. You will begin to be contacted and asked to speak at events and asked for interviews. You will not have to pay for them anymore!

[29]*"Marketing is really just about sharing your passion." Michael Hyatt. Michael S. Hyatt is an American author, podcaster, blogger, speaker, and former chairman and CEO of Thomas Nelson.*

I love this statement as it is so true. You are just sharing what you love doing. And your passion will come across when you begin to speak about it.

[30]*Davis Business Consultants say, "Showing up at events as a speaker will help you generate leads. People will probably walk up to you with questions; you will meet them after the event at the informal part. Your*

---

[29]

[30]

network will grow, and sales often start increasing as a knock-on effect of that sooner or later."

Sponsorship of Events

It is always nice to be able to sponsor an event when someone in the community approaches you. These events tend not to break the bank and are a nice way of giving back to the local community and to be seen as a business willing to support local gatherings. It is good for your company's image and perception.

If you tend not to get involved, it might be worth looking into. They do not cost a lot and it is a good tool for building relationships. You may not get a lot of sales from it but there are other methods for generating sales. These events contribute to the overall image of your business and how people feel about you. Let us look at an example of how it can prove beneficial in the long run. Bob owns a large garden centre selling everything from garden furniture, ornaments and log cabins, to plants, flowers and trees.

The local football team is putting on a fashion show to raise funds for their club. They want to build a new clubhouse with showers, toilets, and a kitchen. They approach Bob to sponsor the event, offering him different sponsorship options from the high end of the scale to the low. But Bob says no, sorry guys, I have no interest in football. The event goes ahead, and most local businesses do their bit and agree to some form of sponsorship. There is a great buzz in the community leading up to the event. Everyone who comes into the garden centre is talking about it. They ask Bob if he is going. Bob says no, he has other things on. Bob's wife, however, is keen to go, and so are his kids. But Bob feels uncomfortable as he did not sponsor the event, said he had no interest, so he feels he cannot really attend himself. But his family attend. The community thinks it is odd that Bob doesn't go when everyone in the community is attending, even his whole family.

Then someone calls Bob "a miserable git"; he would not pay for the ticket. Then someone else says, "He wouldn't even buy a raffle ticket for the night, that chap." Soon word spreads around about how Bob would not sponsor the local event and wouldn't even buy a ticket to go on the night. People are not happy. There are over five hundred people at this event. And people talk. Roll on the good weather. Susan says to her husband, Joe, " Oh, we need a new lawnmower; our old one is no use anymore. And we could do with a wheelbarrow and a few other bits." And Joe replies, "Grand, I'll head to Woodies DIY in town; I'm not giving that Bob chap a penny, tight git, he wouldn't even buy a raffle ticket for the Football Fundraiser."

Although this is just one sale there will be many others from the fundraiser who feels the same. So, when all these local people who would usually buy their garden supplies from Bob decide to go somewhere else, it can add up and prove very detrimental. Bob depended on the locals for the summer pick up, as he usually does very well. You can see now how something you think is so small could have such a large effect on your business.

Larger events are different. Sponsoring large events can be very costly and they will generally not provide immediate sales. They are more of a brand awareness tool to generate recognition for your company, who you are, and what you do. Sponsoring large events are an excellent tool for perception. But the difficulty with perception is, it does not turn in to sales straight away. It can, therefore, be difficult to judge whether it is worth it or not. However, if you have the budgets to do it, then do it.

If you feel the event is very beneficial for your industry, ask for the sponsorship packages. Choose one that you can afford and throw yourself wholly into the event and maximize your given opportunities.

For example, you might have your logo on the event website amongst all their promotional material. You could have a few lines about your business for attendees to see. There could be large screens around the whole venue where they have offered to put your logo on and lots more. Read what you will get and utilize every opportunity.

Sometimes a company sends in their logo but they do not include anything about the company, any images for the big screens or any branded items that the event has offered to include in a goody bag for everyone. There are so many opportunities to reach your target audience in different ways at these events.

Maximizing your investment will make for more favourable results than if you were just to send them your logo. Then review the event afterwards. See what contacts you made. Review whether it was worth it business-wise. And if it was, do a deal with the organizer for a package for next year. You can get good discounts by booking a year in advance. And up the value of your sponsorship this time.

Once the event organizers start to promote the event to your industry, your logo will be included from day one on all marketing material going out to the public. And that is added exposure for you.

Chapter Eleven – The Value Chain

Consistency and Alignment

When carrying out a campaign, always ensure that each of your platforms are aligned—both on and offline. For example, going back to the paint shop. If I am running adverts online or on the radio, advertising that we are selling paint at 50% off all day Saturday, have instore signage consistent with the online adverts and ensure that all the shop staff are aware that this promotion is happening. There is nothing worse than walking into a shop or store where you believe there is a promotion, and yet see no sign of it anywhere.

You start to question if there really is a promotion. You might ask someone who works there about it, and then they might have to ask someone else as they do not know. By this stage, most potential customers leave. People usually prefer to see a sign confirming their assumptions rather than have to ask.

Another example is scrolling through your phone, and an advert pops up for a sports shop running a 20% discount for today only. You are interested. The sports company did their homework and targeted you specifically because they knew you liked sport and purchase sports-related products online.

You click the link and go to the site. However, you see no mention of the 20% promotion. You browse anyway and add something to the cart to see if the 20% will appear or be applied then. But, alas, it does not. What do you do?

Number one – you most likely leave the site without purchasing anything.

Number two – the next time you see an advert for this sports company, you will most likely ignore it due to your previous experience.

But why did this happen? Communication is key!

When running a promotion, absolutely everybody in the company must be aware of it. From accounts to purchasing, to customer service, to management to administration, everyone must be aware.

What can happen? Here are a few different scenarios:

- ❖ Website Management Team – Discount not applied to the website, so the online promotion was affected
- ❖ Customer service – Incoming calls asking about the promotion, but staff cannot tell them anything
- ❖ Administration – Incoming calls asking about promotion
- ❖ Reception – Incoming calls asking about the promotion
- ❖ Accounts – Wondering why the sudden increase in sales but at a lower cost.
- ❖ Operations – totally unprepared for the level of demand and therefore go out of stock quickly, bringing an end to the promotion.

This can leave a bad vibe within the company. Everyone is feeling frustrated, and most likely, many potential customers are extremely annoyed if their orders cannot be met. Communication is so important, which brings me to the value chain.

The Value Chain – The Engine

This part would not usually come under "Marketing" but I strongly believe that without an efficient value chain in place, spending budgets on marketing is a waste of time in the long run. I refer to the value chain as "the engine". It is what makes your business tick; it is what keeps the business flowing. It is what pays people's wages, it is what sends out invoices, it is what answers the phones, it is what deals with customers efficiently, it is what manages stock control, it is what organizes the deliveries; basically, it is everything. If you do not look after your engine, your company will begin to break down. Cracks will start to show in different departments, deliveries will be late, invoices will be lost, phones will go unanswered, staff will be sick, wages will be late, emails will go into orbit. The list can go on and on. Before you attempt to spend anything on marketing, you must make sure your engine is running smoothly. Why shine the spotlight on your company if you are not running a smooth ship?

When things begin to break down, the effects are passed on to the customers. This portrays your business in a poor light, therefore creating a negative experience for the customer, which will penetrate out to your community.

If you commit to an investment in marketing, the aim being to drive people to your website or shop, you want to ensure that when they do arrive, you are ready for them.

All departments should be synchronized, so to speak. For example, today, if you ordered a product online, let us say a toy from a toy shop, what would the customer experience be? Think of the journey from the actual browsing experience, to the selection, the add to the basket, the checkout, the order confirmation, the follow-up email, then another email a couple of days later advising the order has been dispatched, then an email from the courier to say it is on its way and then finally it is delivered to your door. There are numerous people or departments behind this journey, all working together to get your order to you on time. But these departments must be synchronized and have a good system in place—the value chain. The path that a product or service follows from when it enters the business to the time it exits.

As the product or service progresses along the value chain, it should gain value, allowing the company to turn a profit by the time the product or service is finally delivered to the consumer. Now, why am I talking about this? Because many companies have internal issues.

Lack of communication is usually the number one reason there is a break down in the value chain. Maybe the price of the product had changed, but the website had not been updated, meaning the customer got the product cheaper, leaving the company worse off financially and someone in trouble. Or maybe when the order went through, the operations department never received it. Perhaps marketing decided to run a promotion and did not tell stock control or operations, leading to shortages in stock and extra staff were needed to keep up with orders. This can lead to frustration and arguments, and more mistakes can begin to occur.

Another example: a sales rep has a new customer on board and sends the information to accounts, forgetting to add in the negotiated deal price. Accounts set them up at the normal rate, and then when the invoice goes out to the new customer, they get really annoyed as they are charged a price higher than agreed, which leads to unnecessary bother and annoyance. It might get sorted out straight away for the customer, but it has still given him or her a negative experience. Accounts will be frustrated with the sales rep for leaving out the price and then there is the question, of whether the price offered had been approved by the powers that be!

Another example: a sales rep secures a new account for a software company. Once they receive the sale, they pass the project's details to the project manager assigned to the client.

However, the project manager is looking at the package sold, shaking her head. No one consulted her for her opinions on what the client needed or asked her for realistic timelines. What has been given to her is near impossible. She knows that not only does the client need extra resources included to complete the project, but that the timelines are not achievable given their current workload. This leads to arguments with the sales team, which then escalate again to the powers that be to sort out. The company could lose out financially if they have to add in extras for free, and the client will get extremely annoyed when they realize the timelines will not be met.[31] A 2015 *survey found that "42% of Americans will stop shopping with a brand that they are loyal to after two bad experiences,"* This is from an article by *Annex Cloud, which is a leading customer loyalty platform.*

A clear communications strategy for your internal team is extremely important. Create a step-by-step process; no matter how simple it looks, create a template that must be adhered to before a new client is signed up. Include things such as: "Has the project manager been briefed? Has the cost been agreed with accounts? Has the workload been agreed by the project teams?" etc. Whatever is relevant to your business to ensure a smooth flow. This way, when there is a problem, you can check the template and see where the communication broke down. By doing this, you will find staff will be more willing to stick to the system. They know that the buck will stop with them and so may be more inclined to ensure they do it right. It will lead to fewer arguments and therefore more harmony within departments.

Office politics can also hamper production. "She can just wait; if she thinks I am doing it now just because she said so, she can take a running jump!" "Who does he think he is? He is not my boss. I will do it my way. The way I have always done it, and he can go take a jump!" "I'm not doing it. I don't care; it's not part of my job." Most companies around the world experience statements like this at some stage. However, controlled by attempting to bring people together.

31

Team Building

Team building events can be a great way of boosting morale and pave the way to strengthen working relationships. Do some research and choose a company that you believe is most suitable for your business.

Be honest with the event organizer about any internal conflict you think there might be. Maybe marketing and accounts do not get on, or maybe sales and operations do not get on. It could be just specific people do not hit it off. It is a good way of putting these people on teams together for the day. Yes, they will likely not be happy having to work with someone they are not particularly fond of, but usually, they will get on well by the end of the day. And they will probably find that they like each other. Also, if your company has a vision, it is good to drive that home at the event. Explain the company's vision and goals, and that they can only be achieved by everyone working together. Get everyone's buy-in.

Staff being asked their opinions and feedback makes them feel much more valued and willing to invest a bit more in the company. It is beneficial to mix teams on the day across departments. You will find they will enjoy themselves and develop a stronger bond with the company.

They will make new friends while strengthening otherwise strained relationships. This is an excellent strategic move for you as it will bring more productivity from the staff, which leads to more profitability in the long run.

[32] *According to High Speed Training, an information and resource site, good communication is essential for great team performance. Team building helps to break down barriers in communication, especially between management and team members. By showing you're*

---

[32]

approachable, employees are more likely to come to you with any problems that arise.

Value Chain Analysis

So how do I start a value chain analysis? What do I do? Let us take a look. As always, I am trying to keep it simple, and you should keep it simple too.

1. Carry out an analysis of the company's current value chain. Start by taking note of the whole process from how your customers find out about your product, to the ordering process, to the operational process, to the dispatch, etc. Consider how all departments or people influence the journey.
2. Make a note of what you have found. This will help highlight to you any issues there may be internally.
3. SWOT Analysis. This looks at your Strengths, Weaknesses, Opportunities, and Threats.

Examples

   a. *Strengths* – great brand name, loyal customer base, great sales team.
   b. *Weaknesses* – the phone is not always answered if very busy with calls, orders can take up to three days instead of two unless the staff is at full capacity, the website is very poor.
   c. *Opportunities* – could look at increasing staff, leading to increased sales as the phone would always be answered, and increased turnaround times would ensure happy customers all round. Could look at improving website which would also bring in more sales.

d. *Threats* – new entrants into the market, competitors lowering pricing, delayed deliveries giving a bad reputation.

These are just a few examples under each heading to give you an idea of what you should look at it.

This is an excellent tool to help you see opportunities you may not have thought of before. You can then put an action plan in place to tackle the issues and go after the opportunities.

[33]Investopedia, an investing and financial education website, states that *"If a company can create efficiencies by analyzing one or more of the five primary value chain activities, it can gain a competitive edge and boost overall profits."*

Benefits of the Value Chain and SWOT analysis:

➢ Improved proposals and products – improves your ability to capture, track and manage customer and marketing requirements to put together better proposals that are more cost-effective.

➢ Better product planning, research, and development. Good value chain management includes working together to maximize synergies across departments. This can help contribute to cost reduction and improved product quality.

➢ By standardizing processes, you are contributing to reducing overall operational inefficiencies and waste.

33

> Reduces costs as optimizing all the value chain components can result in substantial end-to-end cost savings from streamlined processes, reduced inefficiencies and waste, better inventory control, and improved product quality.

> The ultimate result of an effective Value Chain Model is improved profitability.

[34]*The graph below shows how a value chain is modelled. You can carry out a more detailed assessment if you wish.*

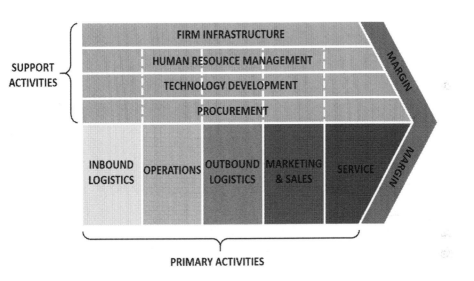

Branded Uniform

If you have staff who are in the public eye regularly, it is important and beneficial to wear branded company clothing, be it a branded polo shirt, a branded jacket, or even a branded hat. It is a great chance to advertise without a huge cost, other than the initial items you have to purchase. It also gives off the impression that you are a professional organization.

[35]*First impressions are vital; and your customers view you differently when your team displays a professional image. Having a uniform that matches your quality of work can lead to consumer confidence.* Model Apparel, a leading uniform supplier.

Leaflet Drops

Leaflet drops can be very effective if, like everything else, they are carried out correctly. This can work for both Business to Business and Business to Consumer. Marketing works best when it is done in alignment. If you just create a leaflet, carry out a local door drop, and hope for the best, you most likely will not get the results you wanted.

However, if you sit down and create a campaign to support your leaflet drop, you will get better results.

When you have worked out the campaign's objective, what you are hoping to achieve, and who your target audience are, make sure to update your digital presence to support this. If someone receives your leaflet through the door and visits your website or your Facebook page as a result, you need to make sure the same information that

---

35

was on the leaflet is on your website and social media platforms. Update all your digital assets with a promotional box, or advert, whatever way you wish to display it. Just make sure it is visible.

You need to be consistent across all platforms. And that won't cost anything extra, just some time. To take it a step further, you could do some social media adverts in conjunction with the leaflet drop so that your adverts will appear to people in the same geographical area as where the door drop was carried out.

If it is a localized campaign, you could take it further again, depending on what results you are hoping for. If you intend to do a leaflet drop as part of a large campaign, then take some adverts in the local newspaper and maybe the local radio station. Consider this: I get your leaflet through the door, which I may only glance at. I am in my car later that day and hear your advert on the radio and make the connection with the earlier leaflet. I go home and read the paper and see another advert for the same, and think to myself, "They seem to be everywhere." I am scrolling through my phone, and suddenly an advert pops up advertising your company and products! And now I click it because I have seen and heard so much about it.

Even if I don't click on it, the product or service will stay in my mind and when there is a time that I need the product, your company will likely be the first one I think of. You may not see the payoff straight away, but you will in time. These types of local campaigns can be very successful, and if they apply to your business, you should look at doing one every quarter for a two-week period. You must ensure that the adverts have the right images and messages on them. Do not overload with information and use good quality material to make them look professional.

Customer Relationship Management / Loyalty Programs

When we do business with people regularly, we begin to build a rapport. When it comes to our loyal customers who stick with us every time, even when competitors try and poach them with more attractive pricing, it is important to make them feel valued, especially from a Business-to-Business perspective. Annual or biannual events can be a good way of rewarding customers. It may be a golf day, a spa weekend, or a day at the races. Whatever it may be, people love being asked to these types of events, especially when everything is complimentary. It really does add a sense of being valued and strengthens the bond with that company.

It usually falls to marketing to organize these things and I have run many of these events myself. At a launch party for a new venue, we had 2,500 people on the guest list—singers, dancers, magicians, celebrities, showgirls, you them it, we had them. It was the most exciting event I have ever had the pleasure of being involved in but it was hard work—long, long days. I remember having to get up at 3 a.m. to be at a tube station in London for 4 a.m. as we were doing a photoshoot for our advertising campaign. The photos consisted of Vegas showgirls, standing from the top down to the bottom of the escalators. So, it had to be done before the station opened. The event was a brilliant success; while admittedly stressful, I came away with many lessons learned, gained valuable knowledge in marketing and events, and made excellent new relationships in the business world.

I am in no way suggesting that you try and host this sort of party. That was a unique situation. I have organized numerous events for customers in terms of golf outings, race days, concerts and football matches and the feedback from the customers is always great. They are delighted to be there and genuinely are appreciative of the day out. It is an excellent way of building on your existing relationships or forging new ones. And your bottom line will benefit in the long run.

For Business to Consumer, it is nice to show repeat customers that they are valued; most companies have some sort of loyalty program these days. Branded merchandise can be a good way of rewarding Business to Consumer: branded keyrings, pens, or calendars, for example. You are sending customers a gift, but it will have your company name or logo on it, which is good exposure for your company.

Most companies have loyalty schemes that entice the customer to continue to purchase with them. [36]According to an article from Annex Cloud, *"Increasing customer retention helps boost profits simply because loyal customers already have trust in your brand and therefore are likely to spend more. Increasing retention by just 5% through customer loyalty programs can boost revenue by 25 to 95%."*

If you do not already have a loyalty scheme in place, now is the time to do it.

Lead generation campaigns

This is mainly for the Business-to-Business sector, but Business to Consumer could still avail Lead Generation campaigns if they are looking to do deals with other businesses.

Not many people enjoy cold calling or trying to organize meetings with people who are difficult to get a hold of. It can be hard work, time-consuming, and frustrating. If you are in this type of business, I recommend using a telesales company to secure the meetings you require. There are telesales companies specific to every industry, and they have the contact details of the people you need. They are experts at getting to the right person and regularly succeed in arranging meetings with those important to you.

Many will act as a representative from your company to whomever they are speaking to and will be fully briefed in advance so they can

---

answer questions they may be asked. They can arrange three to four quality meetings a week for you if that is what you want. They usually work on a percentage of any business won, so you will not have to pay for a meeting that is set up unless you win business from it.

Obviously, different companies have different structures but it is certainly worth exploring if you are having difficulties speaking to the right people.

Radio

In my experience, the best way to use radio adverts is by running a brand awareness campaign followed by a promotional campaign. If you run promotional adverts independently, with no other marketing activities, you may yield results but not near what you could potentially achieve. You need to build up your presence or image and get people to trust your brand before you start asking them to buy. As mentioned earlier, if you are running a radio campaign in conjunction with digital ads, newspaper ads, and leaflet drops, then you will receive a much better return from your radio campaign.

However, for the most effective way to use the radio, you should build your image first. Sponsor a show or news program, or the weather. Your company and what you do is usually mentioned at the start and end of these shows daily. Or simply do a run of adverts for two or three weeks every quarter. These adverts should not be promotional. They should just be about your company, what you do and contact info.

When it comes to a promotional campaign and people hear your promotional adverts, they will be much happier making a purchase as they are now familiar with your company.

By mixing up your campaigns with brand awareness and promotions, you build trust with your audience, rather than just asking them to buy all the time.

Guerrilla Marketing

Guerrilla marketing is an advertising strategy that uses the element of surprise to promote a product or service. It is when a company does something in public to attract attention. For example, when we were getting ready for the launch campaign for the large venue I spoke of earlier, a few Elvis impersonators and showgirls would set up somewhere on a busy street in London and start dancing to music. Everyone wondered what was going on and were then handed a leaflet about the opening of the new venue. There were several groups of entertainers doing this numerous times over the course of a couple of days. However, while it was an excellent campaign and generated massive interest from local media including popular radio stations, it certainly put a dent in the budget.

Of course, there are some less costly things you can do if you want to stand out from the crowd.

In one company where I worked, there was a Tall Ships Festival Event, where seventy majestic tall ships were arriving in the quayside of an area we had services in. The organizers were expecting up to half a million visitors from all over the country and the world to attend. We investigated doing radio, leaflet drops, newspaper adverts, and the works from an advertising perspective. But then we realized we would only reach the local people with this strategy. We wanted to raise our profile nationally but visitors would likely not see the newspapers, nor hear the radio adverts or get the leaflets. Plus, the cost for all these initiatives had skyrocketed given the size of the event.

So, we decided to go down the guerrilla marketing route and had two eye-catching costumes made. They were wheelie bins with the company brand sewn across the front. They were like cartoon characters in terms of size, such as Mickey Mouse, or Minnie Mouse, so you could not miss them. They walked around, shaking hands, waving at people, and mixing with the crowd. It was the best thing we could have done. We got huge exposure. All the children wanted to get their photos taken, we got in all the local and national press and were even spotted on the TV news several times. The only cost incurred was the costumes and leaflets we had printed up; not to mention the fun we had. Sometimes it really pays off to think outside the box!

Plan for the year head

At times, I know it can be difficult to plan for next week, let alone the year ahead. But it is a good idea to sit down and work out what is coming up in terms of your busy periods, your quiet periods, when you think a campaign would work well, when you have certain events, or perhaps you might have a new product or service coming down the line. Create a calendar for the year and mark off the periods you believe marketing will be most important. Write down those dates, the theme (e.g. Easter, Christmas, Bank Holidays), and allocate a marketing budget to each of these periods. Then you and your team can prepare well in advance and know what you have coming down the line.

This removes any concerns or pressure you may usually feel leading up to such events when trying to organize things last minute. It is also good that you can inform your customers about sales or promotions coming up. You do not have to have the whole promotional details nailed down but knowing the time periods will demonstrate professionalism. You can also start to drip feed details of the upcoming promotion on your social media platforms, which will generate interest early.

Costings and Return on Investment

When committing a budget to marketing, it is very important that we see a return on our investment. When starting out with your strategy, you are likely to spend more and see less as you are trying to establish yourself in the market.

Brand awareness activities do not show an immediate return, and therefore measuring spend against success can be difficult in the short term. However, this does not mean spending budget on campaigns and receiving little in return. Digital campaign performance can all be tracked and evaluated to see if they are worthwhile. Here is what I recommend.

When it comes to promotional advert campaigns, you can usually measure the return, especially for the digital campaigns. For social media and google adverts, you can track the amount you spent on adverts versus the number of products or services you sold or the revenue you generated as a result. Allow the adverts to run for at least a week before you start to analyze. If you are receiving little return for your budget, make sure to take the details of what you did in terms of what headline you used, what imagery you used, who the target audience was, and what platform.

Be mindful of this when creating the next one. Remember, if you are running adverts correctly on social media, you will have numerous different campaigns targeting different audiences. It could be that you are running three adverts on Facebook. Maybe two of them are gaining you little or no engagement and no sales. But the third one has high engagement rates, and you are receiving orders as a result. If this is the case, stop the two underperforming ads and invest more budget in the campaign that is working.

The same goes for any other promotional adverts, be it Google, Twitter, Instagram or YouTube. Promotions are to promote a product in the hope that people make a purchase.

You can get detailed analytics of each of these platforms to see how many people clicked your advert, how many people commented or sent you a message as a result. You can see how many people went to your website. Remember that if you include a link to your website in the advert, the sales could be coming in through there.

You might not receive much engagement in terms of likes, comments, or shares in your advert, but if your sales are up from the website and you can see that people clicked your advert on Facebook, you can be sure that is where the rise in sales is coming from.

When running promotional adverts on the radio, newspaper, or in a leaflet, it is important to include a field on your website ordering form asking where they heard of your company and make this entry field mandatory. It is important that those on the phones who take orders also ask the same. In this way, we can get a good idea of where most of the sales are coming from. If one medium is not getting many mentions, but the other two are getting a lot, drop the one that is not yielding a return and focus more on the ones that do. Trial and error will help you carve out the most cost-effective advertising path for your business.

When it comes to brand awareness, it can be tougher to decipher a cost-effective strategy.

It is a good idea to have quarterly sales targets in place, as reviewing these results will help show if you are on the right road or making any headway. The results from brand awareness activities can take up to a year to come to light. When creating your marketing strategy, commit a specific budget for one year and carry out all the activities that have been included in the marketing plan. Review your market position after the year – your market share, sales, and revenue. If you carried out all the initiatives in a targeted way, you should be pleasantly surprised at your results.

Chapter Thirteen – Competitors

While you do not need to know your competitor's every move or monitor them daily, it is still good to keep watch to ensure you are not missing out or lacking anything that might put you a step behind. It is always beneficial to carry out a competitor's analysis every three to six months, at least. Have a look at your top five competitors.

Check out the following:

- Their Product Offering
- Their Pricing Strategies
- Any added Value
- Their Delivery Processes
- Customer Service Community
- Customer Journey
- Overall Marketing Approach
- Digital strategy
- Website
- Social Media Platforms

Are there any platforms they are on, and you are not? Are there partnerships they have that look beneficial that maybe you could explore?

- Engagement – do they receive much engagement on their posts? Do they get many likes, shares? Retweets? Comments? etc.
- Brand – how do they position themselves in the market? Do they advertise as a market leader? Or as a cheap solution? Or

value for money? Be aware of what they are selling themselves as.

- o Content – what type of content are they putting out there. What is the quality of the content like?
- o Customer service – look at feedback in the community. Are customers generally satisfied with them? Are there any issues?
- o Promotions – what type of promotions do they offer?
- o Email/Push/Text – how often? What is the frequency?
- o Testimonials – do they have customer reviews? What are they like?

If applicable, visit their stores or shops. Have a look around. Take it all in.

What are the staff like? Courteous, knowledgeable, uniformed? What are their displays likes? It can help to create a spreadsheet and keep the information recorded in one place. When you have all this done and analyzed it, you might be surprised to find that you have identified some opportunities you had not thought of before. You might spot a gap or an area where there is more room to grow than you realized. Not only is it a great way to keep an eye on competitor activity and to make sure you are not falling behind, but it could also present you with a new idea that could prove very lucrative.

For example, if your main competitor did not handle customer service very well and had many complaints about deliveries always being late, you could use this as an opportunity. Create a marketing campaign that focuses on how you provide top-class customer service and how your deliveries are always on time. Put in a short testimonial to support this. "Chapley are second to none when it comes to customer service! Always on time. I would never go anywhere else." This could entice your target audience to give your business a chance instead of who they usually use, particularly if they are frustrated with your competitors.

It is also wise to carry out a competitor's analysis on businesses that are not in direct competition with you but still supply similar products.

Maybe you supply to different audiences but have the same concepts. Again, doing this type of research can open gaps in the market that you might not have spotted before. Doing your homework can be beneficial in these circumstances.

Marketing Plans – Where to start?

You may be wondering where you will get all the time to do all of the activities I have outlined, and the truth is you most likely will not, especially if you are trying to run a company or carry out other responsibilities. For SMEs, I would recommend hiring a marketing executive if you do not already have one in place. Why, then, am I reading this book if I can just hire a marketing person to do it? You may ask. The reason I am writing this book is to help you understand marketing, to help you understand the best way to reach your target audiences and the most effective way to generate the largest returns.

It means that you can work closely with your marketing teams and create a marketing strategy together. It means you are fully aware of what the marketing team is doing and can feel a lot more content. A large proportion of the population does not understand marketing or what marketeers "do". There can be much negativity around marketing, in terms of it being a cost which gives nothing back; that it's "just doing a few adverts here and there"; or it's just managing a Facebook page. If there has to be cost-cutting across a company, marketing tends to get cut before everything else.

This should certainly not be the case. I do, however, understand why some companies feel like this. A lot of businesses will hire a marketing person but will have no actual job specification for them.

They understand they need marketing but are not knowledgeable enough about what that role entails or what the tasks should be.

They take on a new hire and expect him or her to come to them with the marketing plan. It may be advertised as "This is a new role that you can carve out yourself". In other words, "We have no idea what you are supposed to be doing." For this to work for the company, you need to have a good understanding of marketing yourself. You can then create a plan, together with the new hire, to carry out the activities needed. The other option is to hire a high-level marketeer who is experienced enough to make it work without your input but these hires will be much more costly and will likely require a large marketing budget. However, there is no point bringing in a marketing person with only a couple of years' experience who does not really understand strategy yet, and perceives social media posting and Google adverts as the answers to everything.

Every marketing campaign should have a strategy. Why are you doing it? What is the goal? What do you want to achieve? What percentage of increase in sales are you looking for? How many new customers are you looking for? Etc. Doing campaigns here and there on the fly or in reaction to the market is why marketing receives a bad name because not having a plan does not yield good results. You then end up spending large budgets on campaigns and receive little or nothing back. So, if the MDs, CEOS, or managers fully understand the fundamentals behind a good marketing strategy, this will help you not only hire the right person, as you will know what questions to ask, but it will also help you with the marketing team. It will help you really buy into the strategy, get you excited and passionate and then you will start seeing the results from your efforts.

Sole traders, however, do not need a full-time marketing person. Try and do what you can yourself and hire some freelancers if you need help. I would advise you to carry out the minimum tasks I have set out in the following chapter laid out specifically for you.

The number one thing every company or business should have is an annual marketing plan broken down by quarter. This should be shared with all departments so everyone is aware of what is happening and when.

This relates to sole traders too. You need to have a plan. Obviously, there will be flexibility, and you might end up not doing some of the things you had intended, but you may do something else instead. It is beneficial to have a plan in place, though, with quarterly targets, and then you can review after three months to see what progress is being made. If you find some of the initiatives you are doing are not proving very successful, then it might be worth switching it out for something else: trial and error. Every business differs, and what works for one may not work for another, even if they are very similar businesses. Try different approaches, monitor the performance, and eventually, you will only be spending your budget on the activities you know will yield a good return.

I am sure you are wondering where to start as there such a lot of information here. While I have included everything that I can help you with, that does not mean that you must do absolutely everything to succeed. Some of the marketing tools will suit companies, and others will not. What works for one may not work for another. Some tools will not be relevant to some industries. However, over time, as your business begins to grow and grow, you will most likely end up doing most of what I have included, but you'll be marketing pro's yourselves by that stage, so do not let the thought scare you!

So, how do you know what you should be doing? I am going to break it down for you, ladies and gentlemen. Let us get started with the sole traders or those who just have a few working for them. I will tell you what you need to do, as in the bare minimum, to get started and moving in the right direction. We have covered everything in detail already. I will, however, elaborate a bit more on some of the previous points and be more specific.

You can always refer to previous chapters if you would like more information on each item. I have included a little direction with each one to help you, though. By now, if you have read to here, you should have a much better understanding of marketing, so you will find the plans easier to decipher. You will likely have thought of many ideas by now; the examples I have given have hopefully made you think about your own situation and what you can do. I recommend reading all the chapters whether you are a sole trader or SME— it might prove beneficial.

Chapter Fourteen – Sole Traders

I have already covered each of the below topics in previous chapters. Please refer back to the information given about each topic, as it will help you create the most effective marketing plan. Now let us go through each task that you should carry out.

1. Budget & Targets

Set an overall objective for your company. In the long run, what is it you are trying to achieve? By having a clear goal, it will help you to create more effective marketing campaigns as you understand now where it is you are striving to go. I recommend assigning a budget to each of the activities so you know in advance what costs are coming up, and you can plan for them. Please make sure to monitor all campaigns that you spend budget on. As mentioned in the Return on Investment section, you should monitor all advert campaigns; drop the ones that are not yielding you a return and focus on the performing ones. Before carrying out digital adverts, set a target of what you want to see in return. For example, if I spend £50 over one week, I want to see twenty enquiries and five conversions (new customers). When starting out, this will be more difficult as you will not know what to expect. But as you continue to run them, you will be able to get more specific when it comes to what targets you want to set.

2. Audience

Who is your audience? Who are you marketing to? Define them, write it down. Create a minimum of three groups.

3. Refresh Logo/Tagline

Do you need to do work on your logo and tagline? If so, now is the time as it needs to be completed before launching your marketing strategy. You might wonder whether, as a sole trader, you really need a tagline. Yes, you do. Start as you mean to go on.

4. Perception

Messages you want to portray. What do you want people to think of when they think of your company? What do you want to be associated with? For example, great quality, excellent customer service, get the job done on time, services you can trust, etc. Write it down.

5. Imagery/Creative

Find new images to use for adverts/marketing materials. Include the messaging you came up with in the previous stage, and your new logo/tagline.

6. Website

Have your website updated and make sure it is user friendly on mobile platforms. There are plenty of budget-conscious solutions out there. There are sites where you can purchase website templates and commission them to input your content.

It is worth getting someone to show you how to use a content management system. If you can use Microsoft Word and put photos up on Facebook, you can use a content management system. They are very user-friendly and it will save you having to pay someone every time you want to make a change. You may simply learn how to amend the text and images–that will get you by a lot of the time. You can get your website person to do the more difficult things.

7. Testimonials

Give six or seven of your good clients a call and get them to agree to a couple of positive lines about your company. You can then place these on your website and use them as posts on social media. You can also use them on marketing materials that you produce.

8. Content Library

Sit down and think of four or five topics that are quite common in your industry and then create content around them. Write a few articles (just a few paragraphs about something), create a few videos, record yourself giving some tips or showcasing the best way to use a product. Put a request out to whoever does your designs and ask them for ten new graphics.

Explain what you are looking for, with the messages you want. So now you have some articles, videos, and images. Make sure you put enough together to do you for a few months. You should then get into the habit of doing this on a set day every month. It makes it much easier to carry out your marketing initiatives, and it means you are staying on track and in alignment with your marketing strategy.

9. Social Media

If you are not already on Facebook and LinkedIn, I would suggest getting them set up now. Perhaps you have pages but maybe do not use them often enough. The majority of your target audience, no matter what industry you are in, are on Facebook. And those of you who are Business to Business only, yes this applies to you too. People work in businesses.

Improve the overall look of your social platforms, be it Instagram, Facebook, Twitter, LinkedIn, etc. Put up your new imagery and start posting regularly. Twice a week, at least. You need to keep your company name out there. Even if you just mention the weather, get a post out there, making sure you have a good mix of videos, articles, product updates, general, etc. Some of the platforms will let you schedule posts so you can sit down and create a month's posts in advance.

This is a great tool when you have a hectic schedule. Facebook and Instagram have scheduling. I do know that if you use a marketing management software like Hootsuite, or HubSpot that you can schedule posts from a centralized platform for LinkedIn. But posting directly on LinkedIn, you cannot schedule ahead. However, knowing how quickly things change in this digital era, they very well could have it by the time you read this.

If you are in an industry that favours Instagram, you should get that up and running, if you have not already. Sectors such as food, travel, beauty, fashion or health— anything to do with lifestyle - this is a must for those categories. And refer back to my section on Instagram for more information to guide you.

Do not overthink things. Some clients or colleagues I have worked with have to think, talk, discuss, brainstorm, have loads of meetings, and whatever else when making decisions

You do not need to do this. Do not overthink your marketing strategy. Do not waste time and resources. Sit down every Monday for an hour, if you must, and write down your marketing tasks for the week. Or better still, do it the previous Friday so it is ready for you Monday and one less job to do. Have them all prepared and ready to go. Then it will not seem such a big chore.

Think about this – you are a sole trader. Those that know you think of you as a sole trader. While you may be very well respected, you are still seen as a small operation because that is how you portray yourself. But once you implement your marketing plan, suddenly, people see really attractive adverts or posts on social media about your products. They see helpful videos, articles, and information on what you provide. They are learning things about you they did not know.

They begin to take you more seriously. They are becoming more and more impressed. Comments will begin to come in: "I didn't realize you did this, or I didn't realize you were able to do that, etc." For those who do not know you, their first impressions will be based on what they see online. After a couple of weeks of seeing your posts on social media, they will check out your website. After reviewing what you have on offer and your social media content, they will not think of you as a small sole trader.

They will think of you as a professional outfit, much bigger than you probably are, but that is good. They will believe you can handle large projects they may have, whereas right now, they might think you aren't big enough to take on the work they have. You are limiting yourself by not showcasing what you can do. If you keep up with regular posting on both LinkedIn, Facebook and Instagram, if applicable, it will absolutely benefit you. Do not question it. Do not ponder it. Do not let it frustrate you because you are not sure what route to go. Just make a decision and run with it. **Just do it.**

10. Facebook Adverts

If you are selling to the general public, you should certainly be running Facebook adverts. They do not break the bank and they bring in results. They are also quite simple to do if you want to try it yourself. Look for "Ad Centre" on your page and take it step by step. Or if you prefer, get someone to manage them for you on a month-to-month basis. Make sure you have four or five different campaigns running. You do not want to target your whole audience with the same adverts. Remember, speak directly to those you are trying to attract.

Create different adverts with different messaging. You can target people by age, sex, demographics, occupation, interests, behaviours, etc. You do not want to pay to show adverts to an audience who is not interested. When you run targeted ads, you are hitting your audience with messages that interest them, which get them intrigued, making them want to find out more. If you have four campaigns, you will have four separate audiences created for them.

There will most likely be some cross over, but they will still differ enough to need a different message to hook them. Try and include a "Message Us Now" or " Find out more" in the advert so they can send you a message directly concerning the advert. These can work very well for the service and trade industry. For products, "Buy Now" "Shop Now" or "Download Now" are probably more appropriate, depending on what you are advertising. But get someone on board to help (there are lots of freelancers offering Facebook services), explain to them that you want to segment your audience and run targeted campaigns.

Try to be involved, though; do not just hand over responsibility because you assume the advert management company knows what they are doing. They most likely know what they are doing, but they may not be segmenting audiences and could be running generic campaigns.

It is harder work and more time consuming creating multiple campaigns at individual segments, but the results will be far greater and yield a higher return. Any company that provides good Facebook advert management will absolutely run segmented and targeted campaigns.

11. LinkedIn Adverts

LinkedIn adverts are an excellent tool for targeting specific individuals. It can be quite expensive advertising on LinkedIn; Facebook is much cheaper. However, the reason for this is, you can place the content you want right in front of someone who you know is responsible for the next tender contract, or in charge of the next job, or who makes all the decisions relating to purchasing or whatever it may be. You can target people by job title and by what company they work in.

So, imagine you are a plumber or kitchen installer or electrician and you hear that there are to be twenty news houses built in an area you cover. Let's say, Cosgrave Builders, for example, is covering the job.

You can check on LinkedIn if the company has a presence on the platform, and if they do, create content that you want to put in front of them.

For example, write best practices for a plumbing job on estates, or create a video with tips on the best way to approach electrical jobs when there are numerous identical houses to do. Create attractive looking visuals (adverts) with your brand and put in pictures of housing estates with messages like "We can deliver, whether it is one house or twenty." When you create this content, you can then create a campaign on LinkedIn and select only those who work for Cosgrave Builders so that they will be the only people seeing it. This keeps the cost down and ensures your content gets in front of the right person. By continuing to show them relevant content, you are putting your brand in their mind and you are creating a professional image. They may or may not contact you, but you will have a much better chance of securing a meeting than if they had never heard of you.

12. Google Ads

It is beneficial to run Google Ad campaigns to get your brand out there. [37]Some statistics for you:

37

- ➢ 86% of consumers use the internet to find a local business (WebVisible survey).
- ➢ 72% of consumers prefer to find information on local merchants via search.
- ➢ 29% of consumers search for local businesses at least every week.
- ➢ 70% of mobile searchers call a business directly from Google Search.
- ➢ Google Ads convert 50% better than organic traffic.

You can see that it is an extremely beneficial platform. So many people are using it to find businesses like yours every day. It is worth putting in a small budget just to be there, but enough so that you get a few appearances daily. The idea is that when someone Googles "Plumber Dublin" or "Electrician New York" or " Nail Bar London", that your business appears at the top of the page. And while it won't always be there, it will be there enough over time that when someone needs the service or products you provide, they will think of you as they are so used to seeing your brand online. Like in radio, you should just run brand awareness campaigns to start with. Not sell sell—just your business name, what you do, your unique selling points, and a link to your site.

Let your brand build up in people's minds before you hit them with a promotion. But do then hit them with a promotion. If you run a brand awareness campaign for, let us say, a month, then switch up the adverts and start running a promotion on your products or service—be it a special discount, a special offer, a new product—your audience will be more receptive to your promotion because they are used to seeing your company when they Google things related to your industry. They feel they know you somewhat whereas, if they have never heard of you, they most likely will only glance at the promo.

13. Branded Items

Make sure to utilize the tools you have that can act as free advertising. Get your van, car, truck, or whatever it may be, covered with your company brand. Make sure it is done correctly and looks like a professional company. If you want to grow and to generate more business, you have to give the perception that you are operating at a high level with a professionally run operation, regardless of whether it's you on your own or you and one or two others. Remember, perception is key when trying to attract more business.

14. Email.

Normally I would have email much earlier on the list. However, as a sole trader, I think it is more beneficial to get the previous initiatives up and running before you start email campaigns. Email can be a great tool for you to keep in touch with your customers. Get into a routine of sending one email a week, or possibly every two weeks with user-friendly email software. There are plenty out there to choose from. All you have to do after you have created an account is choose a template you like, add your company's logo, add in a few attractive looking pictures related to your business and write a couple of paragraphs of text. The software tool you use will walk you through it, step by step. It is usually a free tool, unless you have a thousand email addresses or more. Again, this is at the time of writing this, so these structures may have changed. Just check it out before creating an account. But by using software like this, it can make your business look very professional.

For example, if I am a window cleaner, I can start to send weekly emails to all my clients, showcasing different windows we have cleaned (permission for photos is a must), news about commercial jobs we might have secured, tips on the best way to clean your own windows, and advising you of a special offer we will have coming up shortly.

You could do a "refer a friend" promotion or run a competition for them. You can go down many avenues when it comes to what content to put in your email. The main thing is that you are in constant contact with your customers and potential customers (if you have emails for prospective clients).

Keeping your brand in the mind of your target audience is key. It will not only help you will maintain your current market share, it will help you increase it.

That is it for now. The table below is a summary of your marketing plan for quick reference.

Strategic Marketing Plan	
1. Budget	8. Testimonials
2. Audience	9. Social Media Posting
3. Logo/Tagline	10. Facebook Adverts
4. Messaging	11. LinkedIn Adverts
5. Images/Creative	12. Google Ads
6. Content Bank	13. Branding
7. Website	14. Email

If you can make the above plan your goal for the next six to twelve months and do it all well, you will certainly begin to see results. When you find a platform that works well for you, keep using it. The more you begin to grow, the more you can start to do more. You could start attending some events, maybe consider doing a local radio, newspaper and leaflet drop campaign supported by social media. When your company has expanded, you can start implementing the extra steps lined out in the next chapter targeted at SMEs.

Let us address each initiative individually.

1. Budget/Targets

Set an overall objective for your company. In the long run, what is it you are trying to achieve? By having a clear goal, it will help you to create more effective marketing campaigns as you understand now where it is you are striving to go. I recommend assigning a budget to each of the activities to know in advance what costs are coming up and, therefore, plan for them. Please make sure to monitor all campaigns that you spend your budget on. As mentioned in the Return on Investment section, monitor all advert campaigns; drop the ones that are not yielding you a return and focus on the performing ones. Ensure you set targets for every campaign even though it may be difficult to start with as you do not know what to expect.

As you continue to run these campaigns, you will have a better understanding of how they work and you will also know how valuable certain results are. For example, you might get twenty enquiries and five sales, or you might get forty enquiries and no sales. However, the enquiries you receive from these campaigns may turn out to be very valuable and you may manage to convert quite a lot of them over time. So, you might assign an enquiry with a high value. However, other companies may receive lots of enquiries but get no business from them which means they would assign a low value to them. There will be a lot of trial and error with your campaigns before you get it right but it is worth it, as once you get it right, your budget will go a long way.

2. Audience

Who are your audience? Who are you marketing to? Define them, write it down. You probably have multiple products and services. It is essential to write down each one separately and a target audience to match. Remember, each target audience will need to be segmented, as one product has more than one audience. People buy your product for different reasons and to speak directly to your customers and get them to buy, you need to segment them into groups. So, rather than confuse things and make it more complicated, I suggest you take your top two products or services and start with them.

3. Perception

This is the messages you want to portray. What do you want people to think of when they your company comes into their mind? What do you want to be associated with? For example, great quality, excellent customer service, get the job done on time, services you can trust, etc. Agree on the messaging for your brand.

4. Refresh Logo

You might have a graphic design company you use, or maybe you have an internal team; get them to come up with a few different examples for your logo. Make what you want explicit. What messages do you want to portray? What do you want to be associated with? For example, great quality, excellent customer service, get the job done on time, services you can trust, etc. Communicate this to the design team.

5. Tagline

Do you have one? Does it need to be changed? If you are going to come up with a new one or amend the current tagline, it is good to get the staff involved. It makes them feel valued when you ask for their opinions. Create a shortlist of three or four that you really like and feel represent the company. Get the tagline incorporated into the new logo show the options with the new logo concepts. Share it across your company and see what the feedback is like. It's good for company morale and will also help you select the most popular one.

6. Imagery/Creative

Find new images to be used for adverts/marketing materials. Include the messaging you came up with in the previous stage together with your amended logo and tagline if applicable.

7. Website

It is important to update your website with the best practices and make sure it is user-friendly on mobile devices. There are plenty of budget-conscious solutions out there.

There are sites where you can purchase a template you like and commission the seller to input all the content.

Get someone in the office to take over the content management system of the website. If you have a marketing team, sit down together, discuss what changes the website needs, and make a project plan for it – goals, tasks, action lists, responsible, etc. Your website is so important; please do not underestimate this.

8. Testimonials

You may already have these, but if you do, get more! Perhaps try and get a testimonials from well-known brands; use these as social media posts and on marketing materials. They are great for instilling confidence in your product.

If you do not already have any, give nine or ten of your good clients a call and get them to agree to a couple of positive lines about your company. Also, put up a list of "Partners" if relevant. Include these logos on your site. It also helps add credibility.

9. Content Library

If you have a marketing team or person, hand this job to one of them to coordinate. You will still have to give input but let them manage the process, come up with the topics and the content format to use. However, if you do not have a team, you will have to do it yourself. Give yourself some time to sit down and think of four or five topics that are quite common in your industry and then create content around them.

Write a few articles (just a few paragraphs about something), create a few videos, record yourself giving some tips, or showcasing the best way to use a product. Put a request out to whoever does your designs and ask them for ten new graphics. Explain what you are looking for, with the messages you want. Now you have some articles, whitepapers (if applicable), videos, and images which are ready to go. Try to put enough together for a month or two.

You should then get into the habit of doing this on a set day every month. It makes it much easier to carry out your marketing initiatives, and it keeps you on track and in alignment with your marketing strategy. Content is SO important. Consistent content. Keep it going.

10. Email

If you have not already got an email software, you need to get one set up. Some software is free if the email addresses are less than a specified number. If you have more than this, there will be a fee every month. There are usually hundreds of templates to choose from, then you add your company logo and information.

However, I recommend that you get a template designed specifically for your business which is relatively cheap to do. Your website company or graphic designer can help with this if they cannot do it themselves. If you simply want a branded template that is compatible with Mailchimp, for example, they can upload it to the software. Every time you send an email, you do not have to keep adding the same company details or editing old templates, you can just use your branded one every time. It looks very professional and it means every email will be consistent and aligned.

Once you have decided on your template, you need to do a little bit of research on how often you should be sending emails. It will depend on your company type and industry sector. There are loads of statistics out there, so use them. It is better to get it right from the start than get it wrong and continually amend your strategy. Plus, you want to get it right with your audience and keep them on side.

Now we have created our template and decided on frequency, the next step is to segment our database. You should already have identified your different segments. As much as you can, split them into databases and name them appropriately. Remember that there can be segments within segments. How far you choose to go is up to you—the further you go, the higher the return. However, for this example, we will look at three segments. If my business is payroll software, I will segment to small businesses, medium businesses and larger corporations. All I need now is the content— be sure to add content relevant to each of the target lists and arrange to send them out as per your email schedule. Please also refer back to the section where I wrote about email to help you create the most effective strategy.

While segmenting to small, medium, and large, it would be even more effective if you were to split them further after that, into sectors. For example, if your payroll software is used by several different sectors, you can use content to speak directly to them, like including top tips for using the software in the retail industry or how your software works best in the production sector. I would suggest starting with a small number of segments, though. You can build these up over time.

11. Push Notifications

This is only relevant if your business has an app where you can make purchases. If you do not already have a push notification strategy, you need one. They are extremely effective and can prove very fruitful. If you are using a specific push note software or your own in-house model, it is imperative that you create, like email, segments within segments.

Create a schedule for each segment, content relevant to each audience, and have a monthly plan, so you know in advance what is coming up. Tie in your push note strategy with your email strategy so they are consistent and aligned. Please refer back to the push note section I spoke about earlier to help you create the most effective strategy.

12. Social Media

I strongly recommend if you are not already on Facebook and LinkedIn, that you get them set up now. It is possible that you have pages but maybe do not use them often enough. Maybe you are using them but do not see much traction from them. Anyway, whatever your situation, social media platforms should be up to scratch and sharing the right posts and content. The majority of your target audience, no matter what industry you are in, are on Facebook. And those of you who are Business to Business only, yes, this applies to you also.

People work in businesses and these people you are targeting most likely have Facebook profiles. Improve the overall look of your social platforms be it Instagram, Facebook, Twitter or LinkedIn. Put up your new imagery and start posting regularly, twice a week, at least. You need to keep your company name out there. Even if you just mention the weather, get a post out there. As long as you have a good mix of videos, articles, product updates, general, etc. Some of the platforms, e.g. Facebook and Instagram will let you schedule posts so you can sit down and do a month in advance which really helps when you have a busy schedule. It is important to have an active Instagram account if you are in the food, travel, beauty, fashion or health industry.

Hopefully, you have a marketing team and will not have to manage this on your own. Work closely with the team if you can but if you don't, do not overthink it.

Sit down at the start of each week and write down your marketing tasks. Have them all prepared and ready to go. Then it won't seem such a big chore.

Think of those in your Industry. Think of your most successful competitors. Are they on social media? Do they have a good digital presence? I am sure they do. Maybe some have been lucky and managed to do well without one, but it will most likely not last.

How are you currently viewed in the market compared with others? Are you seen a leader? Or a follower? Do you wait and see what your competitors are doing, and then follow suit? Do not be this company or business. Do your own thing. Be proactive. Be the leader. I am not saying that you shouldn't keep an eye on what your competition is doing and make sure you are doing as they are and more, but don't leave it to them to test the waters on new initiatives. You test them out. If you try something and it fails, big deal; learn from it, move on, and try the next thing.

If you want to be seen as a market leader, you have to become one. Perception is key. Put yourself out there. If you were THE number one market leader in your industry and let us say your budget was not an issue, would you be doing anything differently? Maybe you would like to try new things at the minute, but you would rather wait until you have grown a bit more. Do not wait. Do it now. Why wait until you are up there? Do it now and you will get you there much quicker.

Thinking again about your social media strategy, once you implement this plan, people will start engaging with your adverts or posts on social media about your products. There will see helpful videos, articles, and information on what you provide and will start learning things about you they did not know. They will begin to take you more seriously and become more and more impressed. Comments will begin to come in, "I didn't realize you did this, or I didn't realize you were able to do that, etc.".

First impressions will be based on what people see online for those who do not know you. After a couple of weeks of seeing your posts on social media, they check out your website. After reviewing your website and your social media content, they will not think of you as a small business. They will think of you as a professional outfit, much bigger than you probably are, but that is good. They will believe you can handle large projects they may have, whereas right now, they might think you aren't big enough to take on the work they have. Let people know how knowledgeable you are. Let people know what you can do. You are limiting yourself by not showcasing what you can do. If you keep up with regular posting on both LinkedIn, Facebook and Instagram (where applicable) it will absolutely benefit you. Don't question it; just do it.

13. Facebook Adverts

These will be very helpful in the Business-to-Consumer market. These adverts do not break the bank, and they bring in results. Depending on the type of person you are or your situation, you might like to try them yourself. If you would, please refer back to Facebook Adverts in the Sole Trader chapter, where I have provided some guidelines on how to go about it.

However, if you are an SME you probably have a marketing person or team on board. If you don't, there are lots of freelancers offering Facebook services who could help. You must make it clear to whoever it is that you want to segment your audience and run targeted campaigns. Do not just let them take over because you assume they know what they are doing. They must understand what you want in terms of segmenting audiences and running generic campaigns. Make sure you segment and target those segments with messages relevant to them. There is a lot more work involved in creating multiple campaigns at individual segments, but the results will be far greater and yield a higher return.

14. LinkedIn Adverts

LinkedIn adverts are excellent for targeting specific individuals although it can be quite expensive; Facebook is a lot cheaper. However, the reason for this is that you can place the content you want right in front of someone who you know is responsible for the next tender, or in charge of the next job, or who makes all the decisions relating to purchasing.

This type of campaign can prove extremely beneficial for SMEs. You can target people by job title and by what company they actually work in. Target the project manager, operations manager, chief engineer, purchaser, whoever they may be.

For example, imagine you are a specialized building contractor and hear Pfizer, the pharmaceutical giant, have just received permission to build a massive new building within your target area. There will be several building contractors involved and you would love to be one of them. You can start creating content that you know they would be interested in and place this content in front of them. For example, you could create a video with tips on the best way to approach the type of building that they plan on creating; you could write an article on issues or problems these types of building usually throw up; you could create engaging visuals demonstrating what you do, and why you are the best at what you do. Make it specifically relevant to what they intend to build. When you can put this content right in front of them, they will not know that you created it specifically for them, they will just believe they are standard adverts across the platform. If they continue to see your content, and it is really good, you might get a phone call. If you do not, after a few weeks, lift the phone and put in a call. They will most likely speak to you as they not only now know who you are, but they know that you are knowledgeable.

Even if the jobs have already been awarded to someone, you have made contact, and you could likely be on the next tender list.

Think of ten to twenty different companies that you believe you could help. Perhaps they have given out larger contracts to your competitors, which is very frustrating as you believe you can do a much better job. This is your opportunity. Find out what each contract entails and build content around it. Place the content in front of the decision-makers or even select employees from the whole company. When you create this content, you can then create a campaign on LinkedIn and select only those who work for the company in question so that they will be the only ones seeing it. This keeps the cost down and ensures your content gets in front of the right person.

By continuing to show them content relevant to them, you are putting your brand in their mind and you are creating a professional image. They may or may not contact you, but you will have a much better chance of securing a meeting than if they had never heard of you! You are building your credibility and building a connection with them.

And over time, you will be surprised when you start getting calls out of the blue from top companies who have been "keeping an eye on you".

15. Google Ads

It is beneficial to run campaigns on the Google Ads platform to get your brand out there. Include a monthly budget for them, enough that you get a good few appearance on a daily basis. You do not have to spend a lot here. The idea is that when someone Googles your services or anything related to it, you appear at the top. Let us take a building contractor, for example. Use the keywords associated with your business and whenever someone Googles building contractors, you will be there—not every time—but enough to get noticed.

Let your brand build up in people's minds before you hit them with a promotion. But then do hit them with a promotion. If you run a brand awareness campaign for a month, switch up the adverts, and start running a promotion on your products or service. Be it a special discount, a special offer, or a new product, your audience will be more receptive to your promotion because they are used to seeing your company when they Google things related to your industry. They will feel they know you a little whereas, if they have never heard of you, they most likely will only glance at the promo.

16. Branded Items

Make sure to utilize the tools you have that can act as free advertising. Get your vans, cars, trucks, or whatever it may be, covered with your company brand. Make sure it is done correctly and looks like a professional company.

If you want to grow and to generate more business, you must give the perception that you are a professional operation. Remember, perception is key in attracting more business—particularity for larger contracts and securing tenders.

17. Magazines/Newspaper Interviews

It is worth securing an interview or feature in a magazine related to your industry. It has great potential to raise your profile, and it will put you on the path to becoming a market leader. It can unleash opportunities that you might have never realized were there.

18. Press Releases

I would recommend doing press releases, especially if you are a medium size business. Refer back to my paragraph on Press Releases and try to commit to doing one every six to eight weeks.

19. Webinars

Depending on the type of business you are in, arranging webinars could be beneficial. One every four to six weeks to start with but in the long run, you should be doing one every couple of weeks, at least. You need to create momentum and build it up. They need to be marketed properly. Send out an email and share them on your social media platforms; get your staff to tell customers and potential customers about them; have them listed on your website. Include a promo at the bottom of the company email signature with the schedule for webinars.

If you have a big team, assign this to someone to run and manage. Get them to do the webinars and start sending emails to advertise them three weeks in advance. Give people a chance to register in plenty of time. Always send an email to those who registered afterwards whether they turned up for it or not.

20. Telesales Lead Generation Campaigns

These campaigns can enable you get some lucrative meetings set up and get your foot in the door to the really big companies. They all operate different payment structures. Some might be a percentage of business won; some might be an actual figure for a meeting secured; some could be a fee for every meeting regardless of whether won or not. Some of the structures can be confusing.

Ensure you agree on a payment structure that will be easy to calculate when the time comes for payment. There needs to be a clear definition of what merits payment and how much. But aside from this, these companies can be excellent. If you are struggling to get into the top ten companies, and if you can't seem to make headway, you should try using them. However, if you are carrying out all that I have advised, you should certainly already be on your prospective client's radar.

I am, therefore, not suggesting that you run out and do this But you should assess the situation. If you think it could be a worthwhile strategy, do not jump in straight away. Wait until you have your website, social media platforms, and digital presence aligned with relevant content and consistent messaging. You want to make sure that if these targets Google you, that you look very attractive to them.

21. Events

Attending events that are relevant to your business would be beneficial.

Try and secure a stand so that you have a presence there. But more importantly, make sure you secure a speaking slot in the deal, even if it is on a panel discussion. If you are not someone who has spoken before or spoken much, it would be a good idea to start with a panel discussion. Usually, there will be three or four people discussing a specific topic and answering questions together.

Becoming a market leader means being perceived as a market leader. How can you be seen as a leader if your company has no representation for the whole seminar? The speaking slots are filled with your competitors and other related businesses in the industry. Becoming a regular speaker will help you to be seen as a market leader.

Make a list of must-attend events for your business and then create a second list of not so important events, although it would be good to be there. Either you or someone in the office, should contact all these event organizers individually regardless of when the event is. The earlier you get in, the better speaking slot choice you have. Book them all in advance if you can so that you know what you have coming up which will help you to prepare.

For the not quite so important events in the second list, make a note of the contact for each one, and when it gets closer to the time contact the organizers, and you may get a last-minute deal at a favourable price.

22. Radio

Radio adverting has had a difficult time in this new technological era. With digital advertising being so trackable and results being so transferable, radio struggles to prove itself. For me, radio can be very beneficial but it must be used in the right way. If you are operating locally and nationally, you should be using radio. However, do not just do ad hoc campaigns – have a strategic plan in place. Promotional adverts should only be used as part of an overall campaign where you are doing other things. If you have no promotion campaign going and are advertising on radio, it should be about brand awareness. Sponsor a show, the weather, or a business show and speak to the radio company about raising your profile. The representative will usually have lots of different options and know what a good fit for your business is.

Focus on raising your profile and only use promotional adverts when you are doing an overall marketing campaign. Getting your website and social media platforms up to scratch, your content bank created and making sure your digital footprint looks good are more important to have done first. Once you are all singing and dancing, then look at some opportunities for radio. Just make sure whatever you decide to do on the radio ties in with your overall marketing strategy and that your website and social media presence reflects the same information.

In one place I worked, we wanted to increase the footfall coming into the venue. We started with brand awareness, doing a full-on campaign. We sponsored a daily business show on a radio station that our target audiences listened to. We secured bus and rail adverts on routes that would reach our audiences, and we carried out some online Google campaigns. We were simply focusing on raising our brand and our services. Then we changed the adverts, from awareness to promotions, adding in local leaflet drops and newspaper adverts.

It worked really well. Our footfall increased tenfold. Everyone was talking about us. Our Facebook followers and engagement rates went through the roof. We were inundated with calls and emails from people wanting to book private events and parties. We certainly saw a return on our investment.

23. Billboards/Bus/Train Adverts

These types of adverts are usually the ones that non marketeers dislike the most. They cost quite a lot to do and there are no trackable results. There no way of telling how many people the advert reached, how many people clicked on it, how many people read the advert, etc. There is no digital footprint which, in today's world, is very uncommon. We can track almost everything. Usually, we are given the average footfall passing a specific billboard, or how many people use the bus service or how many use the carriage on the train where your advert will be shown. It is a difficult one. I love this type of marketing, though; maybe it is the marketeer in me.

Have I found them effective? I have to say, yes, I have, on the few occasions that I have used them. However, it is difficult to tell as I have never run them as stand alone. When I ran these types of campaigns, they were part of an overall campaign. We had many media formats from website, social media, and newspapers to radio and leaflets, etc.

Anytime we have gone the whole hog on a marketing campaign, I have seen excellent results but I cannot say that the billboards were the main reason. They were one of the reasons which certainly helped.

What helps more than anything is consistency. People see your advert online. Then they see it in the local paper. They might hear it on the radio. And then they see this huge billboard with the same advert. Very powerful. Very impactful.

I feel billboards are a strength and can really add value to your marketing campaign although it is not possible to measure the impact of them. It is difficult for marketeers to get approval from the top to run these types of campaigns. As long as they are included as part of an overall campaign, do try and consider them. You can get some great deals on these ad panels, so negotiate.

24. Full-on Campaign Examples

If you have something important coming up that you know you will commit a lot of budget on, like a new product, a whole new side to your business could be a new app, whatever it may be.

Depending on what type of business you have, you will either carry out online campaigns only or do both. For the best results, I would suggest the below table:

Online & Traditional	Online Only
➤ Website	➤ Website
➤ Social media posts	➤ Social media posts
➤ Social media adverts	➤ Social media adverts
➤ Google adverts	➤ Google adverts
➤ Email Campaigns	➤ Email Campaigns
➤ Push Notes/SMS	➤ Industry News Site Takeover
➤ Local newspaper adverts	➤ Video Ad Campaigns
➤ Local radio campaigns	➤ Push Notes/SMS
➤ Leaflet drops	➤ In App Messaging
➤ Billboard advertising	➤ Press Release
➤ Bus advertising	
➤ Train Advertising	
➤ Press Release	

In one company I worked at, we would run a large campaign every bank holiday weekend. Digital media was only beginning to take off then, and the campaigns were very much focused on radio, newspaper, and leaflet drops. We had a massive success rate when we ran these promotions.

The first one got me in hot water as I did not advise operations. In fairness, I did not realize it was going to be so successful. (I have since learned this is no excuse – communication is vital). We ran out of stock the first time we did it. But that is all part of the learning curve. We never ran out again. And we were always flat out every time we did the bank holiday campaigns. It is important to test the water.

Try out different avenues when it comes to doing a full-on promotion. What works for one company may not work for another. But once you find what works, it is so satisfying, as you are committing a budget to a promotion that you know is not only going to deliver but will increase your market share, be cost-effective and, most importantly, generate increased revenues.

25. Customer Relationship Management (CRM)

This is important if you have a loyal following that you class as your bread and butter, so to speak. Companies that never let you down and always put their orders through you. They are not enticed away by competitors undercutting prices and offering attractive deals. Most businesses have several customers that they can rely on. And if that is you, then it is always good to reward them with something such as a day out.

Invite them and their partners golfing or to a spa day, for instance; to a football match with corporate hospitality; take them horse racing, dog racing, or to a Formula One race.

Find out casually what they are interested in, although if you already have good relationships with these people, the chances are you will already know what they are in to. This makes customers feel valued. It also solidifies your relationships with them, making them less likely to leave you, regardless of the situation. Also, depending on what country you live in, it would be worth purchasing annual tickets for individual stadiums. For example, in Ireland, we have the GAA (Gaelic Athletic Association), Gaelic football and Hurling being our two main sports. When our county teams do well in the championship and get to semi-finals and finals, tickets are like gold dust. Soccer is a popular event almost wherever you live and securing annual tickets to several stadiums would certainly put you on favourable terms with your customers. In the USA, baseball and American football would probably be favoured. As people have different preferences, it is important to find out what the majority enjoy as you do not want to commit to a spend in a specific stadium if your customers are not really a fan of the sport. This will not achieve your goal.

The other benefit of acquiring these types of tickets are competitions. This is a great way of getting engagement on social media. I used to do this a lot in one of the companies I worked for. I would put up a post giving away two tickets to an important upcoming GAA match. People had to like and share to qualify. At first, I was quite shocked at the responses. People really do get involved. We would get thousands of likes and shares. It is a great way of building followers and raising your profile.

So here is your plan in a table for reference. Please have a look and tick off those which are applicable to you or your business.

It is time to get started on your journey to becoming **a market leader!**

Strategic Marketing Plan	
1. Budget/Targets	14. LinkedIn Adverts
2. Audience	15. Google Ads
3. Messaging	16. Branded Items
4. Logo	17. Magazine / Newspaper Interview
5. Tagline	
6. Images/Creative	18. Press Release
7. Website	19. Webinar (B2B)
8. Testimonials	20. Telesales Campaigns
9. Content Library	21. Events
10. Email	22. Radio
11. Push Notes	23. Billboards
12. Social Media Posting	24. Full On Campaigns
13. Facebook Adverts	25. CRM

I will not go into detail for each item for these companies as they have large marketing teams and resources and have the expertise in-house to carry out successful campaigns. However, I will offer my views in relation to specific items.

Logo/Tagline

A huge amount of resources usually go into the logo and taglines in larger corporations. They understand the importance of getting it right, and it is something that sometimes takes months for them to agree. The fact that they take it so seriously should be an indicator to the smaller companies out there of the importance of their own logo and tagline.

Messaging/Images/Content Bank

Corporations will have an in-house marketing team but will also work with numerous marketing agencies. They will have meetings upon meetings upon meetings around content and messaging. They will have a huge content bank built up under every relevant topic to their business. Vast amounts of budget are invested in this area, again, highlighting the importance of creating the right image.

Website/App

With such huge resources, the website should be top-notch. However, this is not always the case. I have come across some with websites that can be confusing. Again, keeping it simple is key. And it can be difficult to do this when you offer so many products but too much information on the home page puts people off. There should also certainly be a company app with companies this size, even if you cannot provide sales through it. It is good to have one for account management or company news and updates; whatever way you can make it work, you should.

Testimonials

Larger corporations do not tend to use testimonials as they do not need them. They are giant brands that have made it to the top and so do not need to give reassurance to customers. However, there is no harm in having a testimonial section somewhere on the website or securing testimonials from another large corporation for Business-to-Business opportunities. There is always a potential opportunity to do more. So being prepared and looking your best is key.

Social Media & Digital Ads

The larger companies usually have this nailed. They will have teams upon teams of social media people getting content out on the right channels at the right time. They usually have a presence on all platforms and create lots of content, hoping it will go viral.

Events/Customer Relationship Management

There will be loyalty schemes in place and events for larger customers. They will have tickets to all the major events; they will have days out at the races; they will have weekends away. Larger corporations really home in on the fact that it's much easier to retain customers than acquire new ones.

Customer Service

This is where, in my opinion, a lot of the larger corporations fail. It can be such a trying experience when you have an issue or need to sort something out. They often make it very difficult to speak to anyone. They want you to check out the frequently asked questions on their website and then the online chat or email someone. It can be very frustrating when you cannot speak to a human or, when you do get through, the customer service representative does not really understand what you are trying to tell them.

While marketing has come on so much, I believe companies focus too much on acquiring new customers and not enough on keeping them. In a way, I am contradicting what I said in the customer relationship management section as companies have loyalty schemes and reward larger customers with events and tickets. But in saying that, there seems to be a gap when it comes to customer service.

Think about the times have you phoned a company and been asked for your personal information, like name, address, date of birth, but when you explain what you want and they put you through to someone else, you have to give all that information and explain the issue again. I feel that customer service has gone downwards badly and really needs addressing.

This is not so much the case with SMEs. Most seem to be quite efficient, in fairness. It is the larger bodies. The majority of experience I have had has been really poor, and I hear a lot of the same thing in the community. The inefficiency of staff, the length of time it takes to speak to someone, not being able to deal with queries, constantly having to follow up, and this could be something straightforward like trying to pay a bill. There is a massive need in these large companies to focus on improving customer service. Most of these companies are global. It makes no sense to invest so much money in marketing, acquiring and retaining customers, only to lose them due to poor customer service.

TV

I have not included TV adverts as a recommendation for SMEs as it can be a high cost. If you wish to advertise on TV, make sure your audience can understand the advert. For example, if you are running a national advert campaign, it could be that the actors in the advert have an accent. If this is the case, make sure the accent can be understood clearly. Also, the information being provided needs to be relevant for all geographical areas it is shown in. For example, the US has many states. If your advert appears across all those areas, make sure the actors are speaking clearly and are easy to understand.

You might think this is straightforward, but you would be surprised by some of the material I have been asked to approve for TV campaigns. So, although you may think that the advert sounds great, check out who will be seeing and hearing it, and then make sure people from that audience have seen the advert as you will need their feedback.

With TV adverts it is important to get your audience right. With three young children, I have been subjected to Peppa Pig for six years now. When adverts come on, we want to see them targeted at children to keep them interested. An advert for hair dye targeted at men in their sixties or old age pensioners' cruises are not suitable for a children's channels. Your advert is being totally wasted as the viewers probably don't need a hair dye solution!

You may not even be aware that your advert went out on this channel. It is important to make fully sure of what channels and what times the adverts are going to be shown. You need a breakdown of the audience for each channel, making sure you stick to only the channels you have agreed.

Chapter Seventeen – Conclusion

I wrote this book to help those who either do not have a marketing person in-house or companies who have a marketing person/team but feel that the business is not making progress. And, of course, for those not long on the marketing scene, looking for some direction with their own development. Adapting the strategies I have outlined in the book that apply to your business will help raise your brand awareness, increase your online engagement, increase your market share, and generate larger revenues. It can be done on a small budget.

Obviously, the bigger, the better. Creating content just costs your time, and most likely your own time. Content is the most important part of your marketing strategy. Social media platforms are free. Your website is a free tool. You will have to invest in advert campaigns, getting your website updated, getting professional-looking images, and some other essential items, but we are not talking large budgets here. These can all be done very cost-effectively. Do some research; look at freelancers. Shop around.

But you really cannot afford *not* to do these things. Create your plan based on the essential list I have provided and try and stick to the plan. Please try not to start out with great intentions, only to abandon the marketing strategy when things get too busy or you lose interest. Applying these marketing techniques will absolutely work but only if you carry them out in alignment with each other. Each initiative compliments the other; there is no point in doing a little of this and a little of that. It will not work long term.

You might get short-term gains, but if you truly want to become a market leader, you need to do all that I outlined in the last chapters if it applies to your business. If possible, create your plan with your teams' input. Get them involved. And once you have it completed, share it across the company so everyone knows what the plan is.

Also, please remember, I wrote this book being budget conscious. If your budgets are plentiful, then carry out all the items in this book that apply to your business: use good size budgets for your advert campaigns; sponsor the events that are relevant to you; do as many industry-related interviews as you can; create lots and lots of video content. Do everything I have outlined —you have the advantage of investing larger budgets, and therefore, you will receive better and quicker results.

Please remember the importance of the value chain, your company engine. Make sure it is running smoothly before you launch your new marketing strategy.

Do not expect results immediately, but as soon as your website is ready to go and you start sharing good content, you will begin to see more engagement with your posts, you will start receiving more enquiries, and the level of interest in your business will start to rise. **And this is just the beginning!**

Author

Gráinne Farrell
Strategic Marketing Consultant

Email: grainne@farrell-consultancy.ie

Gráinne is a Strategic Marketing Consultant with nearly twenty years' experience in the Marketing Industry. She has a diverse portfolio at global and national level including gaming, software, energy, insurance and recycling. Gráinne has a first-class degree in Business Management and has been involved in some substantial partnerships including Manchester United Football Club, Ladbrokes, World Series of Poker, Facebook and Google. Gráinne is a certified Digital Marketing Professional, awarded from the Digital Marketing Institute and currently lectures in Digital Marketing at City Colleges Dublin.

References

1 – Strategybeam, a leading marketing consulting firm, states that "defining the target market for your business is the most important piece of digital marketing. By understanding your target market, you can set your marketing efforts and direct your business operations toward success. Target marketing helps your company conserve time and resources."
https://www.strategybeam.com/blog/target-marketing-the-secret-to-business-success/

---

2 – Bryan Eisenberg – "Our jobs as marketers are to understand how the customer wants to buy and help them to do so." - Bryan Eisenberg is a recognized authority and pioneer in online marketing.
https://www.livechat.com/success/great-marketing-quotes/

---

3 – Brian Clark, who is a successful writer and the founder of the pioneering content marketing website, Copy blogger, says, "On average, 8 out of 10 people will read your headline copy, but only 2 out 10 will read the rest." https://copyblogger.com/magnetic-headlines/

---

4 - An article on forbes.com states, "A good tagline helps set you apart from other companies that provide similar products." https://www.forbes.com/sites/theyec/2014/11/03/why-your-company-needs-a-good-tagline/?sh=7ac1192e6d5b

---

5 – Jay Bear, who is one of the world's most inspirational marketing and customer experience keynote speakers and also a New York Times best-

selling author, says, "Grow Your Business by Helping, not Selling".
https://www.jaybaer.com/keynotes/youtility/

---

6 – Michael Brenner – "Content marketing is more than a buzzword. It is the hottest trend in marketing because it is the biggest gap between what buyers want and brands produce." . Michael Brenner is a globally recognized keynote speaker on leadership, culture, and marketing.
https://twitter.com/Statusbrew/status/1180588492998365189

---

7 – According to the eCommerce Foundation, 88% of consumers will research product information before they make a purchase online or in the store. https://theblog.adobe.com/love-email-but-spreading-the-love-other-channels/

---

8 – A study for Forbes in 2018 found that the average user spends 88% more time on a website with video. https://www.oberlo.com/blog/video-marketing-statistics

---

9 – Sumo, a leading provider of pop-up software, carried out research on over 2 billion pop-ups. "If they haven't read two words on your site then how can you expect them to subscribe/buy/do anything for you? Only 8% had pop-ups appear in the 0-4 second mark. And guess what the lowest-converting pages had in common? **Rushed pop-ups.***"*
https://sumo.com/stories/pop-up-statistics

---

10 – Facebook continues to grow every year since it launched in 2004, in both active users and time spent on the platform. It is still the most used

social platform with nearly 2.45 billion monthly active users.
https://sumo.com/stories/pop-up-statistics

---

11 – As Jay Baer also stated, "If content is fire, social media is gasoline."
https://www.doz.com/marketing-resources/social-mediastand-out-tools-instagram

---

12 – 660 million users are on the professional network in more than 200 countries. The platform is also home to over 30 million companies. According to LinkedIn, their growth rate is at two new members joining per second. Among the 660 million LinkedIn members, Europe has over 206 million users. The United States has over 167 million, while the remaining members are from other countries and territories.
https://www.omnicoreagency.com/linkedin-statistics/

---

13 – Twitter is the preferred social network for news consumption. 85% of small and medium business *users use Twitter to **provide customer service**.* 34% of Twitter users *are females and 66% are males.*
https://www.omnicoreagency.com/twitter-statistics/

---

14 – In 2019, the percentage of US adults who use Instagram rose from 35% to 37% and the active reported users have held steady around 1 billion people. https://www.businessofapps.com/data/instagram-statistics/

---

15 – *Kim Garst, who is* an international author and one of the world's most retweeted people among digital marketers, says, "Sell-sell-sell

sales methods simply do not work on social media." https://kimgarst.com/how-to-sell-without-sounding-salesy-on-social-media/

---

16 – *A 2019 study by the Pew Research Center found that YouTube users outnumber those of any other platform in the US, with 73% of US adults identifying as users. Only Facebook, at 69%, comes anywhere near.* https://www.businessofapps.com/data/youtube-statistics/)

---

17 – *According to a survey carried out by Adobe, which looked at how consumers are communicating across email and other channels, time spent checking personal email is up 17% year-over-year. Consumers are checking personal email an average of 2.5 hours on a typical weekday. They also spend an average of 3.1hours checking work email.* https://theblog.adobe.com/love-email-but-spreading-the-love-other-channels/

---

18 – *Below is a graph generated by research carried out by TechnologyAdvice.*
https://technologyadvice.com/blog/marketing/marketing-email-preferences-2015/

---

19 – *According to an article by Segmentify, research indicates the open rates for push note messages is as much as 50% higher than email,* which demonstrates how powerful they can be.

https://www.segmentify.com/blog/five-big-benefits-of-push-notification-in-ecommerce/

---

20 – *In fact, according to Airship, a leading customer engagement platform, a Mobile Engagement Benchmark Survey found that In-App messaging typically receives 8x the direct response rates of push notifications. In combination with push notifications, In-App messages receive an average engagement rate of 26% for a medium-performing app. High-performing apps receive a read rate of 44%, so the opportunity for engagement through In-App messages is high.* https://www.airship.com/resources/explainer/in-app-messaging-explained/

---

21 – According to OutboundEngine, an online marketing software company, acquiring a new customer can cost <u>five times</u> more than retaining an existing customer. https://www.outboundengine.com/blog/customer-retention-marketing-vs-customer-acquisition-marketing/

---

22 – *"About 29% of your attendees won't register for your presentation until the day of the event itself. However, webinar statistics also show that 17% of your attendees will probably sign up more than 15 days before the big day." That* is according to Medium.com, the knowledge platform. https://medium.com/@BigMarker/how-to-effectively-drive-webinar-registration-and-conversions-81057a5be479

---

23 – Studies show that 54% of consumers want to see more video content from a brand or business they support (HubSpot, 2018). https://blog.hubspot.com/marketing/content-trends-preferences

---

24 – Based on the 2018 State of Social Video Marketer Trends report, 73% of consumers claim that they have been influenced by a brand's social media presence when making a purchasing decision. https://animoto.com/blog/business/2018-social-video-marketer-trends

---

25 – A survey conducted by Wyzowl shows that nearly eight out of every ten users have purchased a piece of software or app after having watched the brand's video. https://www.wyzowl.com/video-marketing-statistics-2019/

---

26 – B2B Press, a top PR company, say that "Press releases increase the visibility of your brand in the media. With press release activities planned for the long term, you can improve your recognition and chances of being preferred in the purchasing decision. Press releases enable you to be perceived as an expert in your industry. https://b2press.com/en-US/10-benefits-of-press-release-distribution

---

27 – Testimonials affirm our credibility and trust. Nowadays, this is called social proof. This is according to Vikram Rajana, Forbes Councils Member. https://www.forbes.com/sites/forbescoachescouncil/2017/06/15/top-seven-overlooked-benefits-of-testimonials/#5a66e2561ccd

---

28 – *Agilence, a leading data analytical company, stated "Psychologically, the consumer views the dollar-off promotion as the better deal so the dollar-off promotion is more popular, drives more sales for the targeted item, and increases average basket size, thus achieving the desired goal for the promotion."* https://blog.agilenceinc.com/percent-off-vs.-dollar-discounts-the-psychology-of-promotions

---

29 – *"Marketing is really just about sharing your passion." – Michael Hyatt. Michael S. Hyatt is an American author, podcaster, blogger, speaker, and the former chairman and CEO of Thomas Nelson.* https://michaelhyatt.com/marketing-is-dead/

---

30 – *Davis Business consultants* say, *"Showing up at events as a speaker will help you generate leads. People will probably walk up to you with questions; you will meet them after the event at the informal part; you will exchange formalities,LinkedIn profiles, email addresses, etc. Your network will grow and sales often start increasing as a knock-on effect of that sooner or later."* https://www.davisbusinessconsultants.com/public-speaker/professional-speaking/

---

31 – *In fact, a 2015 survey found that "42% of Americans will stop shopping with a brand that they are loyal to after two bad experiences," states an article from Annex Cloud, which is a leading customer loyalty platform.* https://www.annexcloud.com/blog/10-benefits-implementing-customer-loyalty-program/

---

32 – According to High Speed Training, an information and resource site, good communication is essential for great team performance. Team building helps to break down barriers in communication, especially between management and team members. By showing you're approachable, employees are more likely to come to you with any problems that arise.
https://www.highspeedtraining.co.uk/hub/benefits-of-team-building/#:~:text=Good%20communication%20is%20essential%20for,with%20any%20problems%20that%20arise.

---

33 – Investopedia, an investing and finance education website, state that *If a company can create efficiencies by analyzing one or more of the five primary value chain activities, it can gain a competitive edge and boost overall profits.*
https://www.investopedia.com/ask/answers/061115/what-are-some-advantages-and-disadvantages-value-chain-analysis.asp

---

34 – The graph below shows how a value chain is modelled. You can carry out a more detailed assessment if you wish.
https://www.business-to-you.com/value-chain/

---

35 – *First impressions are vital; and your customers view you differently when your team is displaying a professional image. Having a uniform that matches your quality of work can lead to consumer confidence.*
https://modelapparel.com/7-benefits-employee-uniforms/

---

36 – According to an article from Annex Cloud, *Increasing customer retention helps boost profits simply because loyal customers already have trust in your brand and therefore are likely to spend more. According to the research referenced above, increasing retention by just 5% through customer loyalty programs can boost revenue by 25 to 95%.* https://www.annexcloud.com/blog/10-benefits-implementing-customer-loyalty-program/

---

37 – *86% of consumers use the internet to find a local business (WebVisible survey). 72% of consumers prefer to find information on local merchants via search. 29% of consumers search for local businesses at least every week. 70% of mobile searchers call a business directly from Google Search. Google Ads convert 50% better than organic traffic. (BrightLocal survey).* https://www.mainstreetroi.com/15-stats-that-prove-google-adwords-is-a-great-investment-for-your-business/

Printed in Great Britain
by Amazon